LEARN HOW TO DEAL WITH . . . P6

- WORK PRESSURES
- FAMILY RESPONSIBILITIES
- INFORMATION OVERLOAD
- TELEPHONE TYRANNY
- AND ALL THE OTHER DEMANDS ON YOUR TIME FOR WHICH THERE ARE NEVER ENOUGH HOURS IN A DAY

This remarkable guide, filled with practical wisdom and amazingly simple rules, shows you how to find time to do not only what you *need* to do—but all those things you *want* to do. Organizational expert Ronni Eisenberg has devised innovative strategies for both the office and the home that enable you to do your work with extraordinary efficiency and your chores with no-sweat swiftness.

A clear step-by-step plan along with revealing quizzes shows up such "time traps" as procrastination, perfectionism, self-interruptions, and all those other overwhelming time killers that make you feel harried and hurried. Now, whatever your work load, you can get yourself organized and going with speed tips and time-saving tools that point to 170 new ways to minimize waste, set priorities, make realistic choices, and stay in control. Now, whatever your style or habits, this great resource shows you how to work smarter, not harder. And isn't it about time!

Ronni Eisenberg is a nationally recognized time-management and organizational expert who consults for individuals and major corporations. **Kate Kelly** is a graduate of Smith College and a professional writer. Their bestselling *Organize Yourself!* is a classic in its field.

THE OVERWHELMED PERSON'S GUIDE TO TIME MANAGEMENT

· · · · · · · · · · · · · · ·

Ronni Eisenberg
with Kate Kelly

A PLUME BOOK

PLUME
Published by the Penguin Group
Penguin Books USA Inc., 375 Hudson Street, New York, New York 10014, U.S.A.
Penguin Books Ltd, 27 Wrights Lane, London W8 5TZ, England
Penguin Books Australia Ltd, Ringwood, Victoria, Australia
Penguin Books Canada Ltd, 10 Alcorn Avenue,
Toronto, Ontario, Canada M4V 3B2
Penguin Books (N.Z.) Ltd, 182–190 Wairau Road, Auckland 10, New Zealand

Penguin Books Ltd, Registered Offices: Harmondsworth, Middlesex, England

First published by Plume, an imprint of Dutton Signet,
a division of Penguin Books USA Inc.

First Printing, January, 1997
10 9 8 7 6 5 4 3 2

 REGISTERED TRADEMARK—MARCA REGISTRADA

LIBRARY OF CONGRESS CATALOGING-IN-PUBLICATION DATA:
Eisenberg, Ronni.
    The overwhelmed person's guide to time management / by Ronni
Eisenberg with Kate Kelly.
        p.   cm.
    ISBN 0-452-27682-9
    1. Time management.   I. Kelly, Kate, 1950- .   II. Title.
HN49. T5E57   1997
304.23—dc20   96-36208
                                                     CIP

Printed in the United States of America
Set in New Baskerville
Designed by Eve L. Kirch

BOOKS ARE AVAILABLE AT QUANTITY DISCOUNTS WHEN USED TO PROMOTE
PRODUCTS OR SERVICES. FOR INFORMATION PLEASE WRITE TO PREMIUM
MARKETING DIVISION, PENGUIN BOOKS USA INC., 375 HUDSON STREET, NEW
YORK, NY 10014.

To my most wonderful family, Alan, Julia, Harrison, and Joy, who constantly challenge my organizational wisdom and inspire me to design creative ways to bring order out of chaos.

Thank you for being my family.

—R.E.

To my youngest daughter, Callie, who will never be overwhelmed by anyone or anything. And yes, Callie, I'm finished with the "Interruptions" chapter. You don't have to help me with that anymore.

—K.K.

CONTENTS

· · · · · · · ·

Section 1. A Realistic Look at Time Management

1. Why You're Feeling Overwhelmed   3
2. Just How Time Management Savvy Are You?   11
3. The Importance of Systems   16

Section 2. People, Places, and Things to Do

4. Keeping Track of Places to Be and People to Call:
   Your Daily Planner and Address Book   25
5. Keeping Track of What You Need to Do:
   Your "To Do" List   38

Section 3. Getting It Done . . . and on Time

6. How to Manage the Time You Have:
   Planning and Priorities   45
7. More about Setting Priorities and Finding the Time   67
8. Getting It Done!   80

9. Extra Help, Extra Time: Your Guide to Delegation   96
10. Getting There on Time   110
11. Time-Management Emergencies:
    Coping with the Unexpected   124

Section 4. Helpful Time-Management Systems

12. Errands: Running Them Efficiently
    So They Don't Run You!   131
13. Banking and Bill Paying   142
14. The Mail   157
15. Creating a Filing System That Works   173
16. Computers, the Internet, and Faxes:
    The Information Explosion   183

Section 5. Time Traps

17. Interruptions   201
18. The Two P's: Procrastination and Perfectionism   214
19. The Two T's: Telephone and Television   231
20. Losing Things   249
21. Neatness Counts at Home   260
22. Neatness Counts at the Office   272

Section 6. Speed Tips and Shortcuts

23. 170 Ways to Do Things Better   283

Section 7. Conclusion

24. Staying in Control and Enjoying Your Found Time   307

Section 1

· · · · · · · · · · ·

A Realistic Look at Time Management

CHAPTER 1

. . . .

Why You're Feeling Overwhelmed

It's the nineties, and most people are feeling overwhelmed. Everyone from retirees and young singles to elementary school children and their parents have been tossed into a whirlpool of possibilities—interesting places to go and things to do. The only problem is in choosing.

But all these choices have also made life infinitely more complex. Perhaps what has happened with television is illustrative: Twenty years ago viewers in most of the country selected the programs they wanted to watch from what was offered by one of the three networks. Today those viewers may easily select their evening's entertainment from fifty to sixty programs available through their cable system. Just reading the television listings for the night is a lengthy task!

And television isn't the only part of our lives that has gained in both choice and complexity. The expansion ranges from our work lives to our pleasure pursuits. Today few people work for the same employer all of their lives, leading to the necessity of creating more job options for oneself. Family vacations, which a generation ago might have consisted of a one-week stay at a nearby beach or mountain resort, now may involve anything from flying across the country to visiting a theme park or going on a "dinosaur dig" sponsored by a university.

Children who used to simply attend their neighborhood school now encounter public school districts offering "choice" plans (generally on a space-available basis) that let families select the public school that best suits their child's needs. At times it seems our options are wonderfully endless!

However, opportunity (evening entertainment, job possibilities, family vacations, and school choice, for example) generally comes with a time cost (thoroughly researching the possibilities). Multiply that out across all the parts of your life that have become more complex, and you realize why you're feeling overwhelmed.

Whether we're seven or seventy, we're stimulated and excited by the possibilities, and our first reaction is to try to do everything. Unfortunately, when the day is done, we often feel tired and stressed out. Too many places to be, too many things to do—we just can't fit it all in.

Here are just some of the additional reasons why people are feeling so pressed for time right now.

Juggling or "Too Much to Do. Too Little Time."

Both men and women are assuming a lot of responsibilities. Whether it's a mother splitting herself between home and work, a working father who is also trying to be a more actively involved family member, a retired person who is volunteering around the community while still trying to help out with the grand kids, or a single person traveling on business all week and traveling again to a summer house for the weekend, everyone is trying to do too much, and sooner or later they're bound to be overwhelmed.

The Information Explosion

And what about the ever expanding world of information? A weekday edition of the *New York Times* today contains more information than the average person living in seventeenth-century England would come across in a lifetime! And that's only in a single newspaper. If we consider what is available in books and magazines, it's enough to make anyone sit back in wonder! Should we feel envy or pity for the typical sixth-grader who can now pull more information about the origins of man off the Internet than most college students would use in a term paper?

New Technology

Inventions—ranging from the telephone to the fax machine and the computer—were intended to save time; the reality is that sometimes they actually cost us time by adding urgency. Who can enjoy a calm family dinner with the phone ringing incessantly?

The fax has sped up paper exchange, meaning that certain items that would have been delayed by mail or messenger now often seem to require an immediate response.

And the computer—a definite time saver—also *takes* time by allowing people to expand their commitments; we not only write the flier or invitation, now we design it, too.

As for e-mail, it's like turning on a faucet. Because the system is so well designed for ease of use, messages that previously would never have been sent (no one would have invested postage in them!) now clog up our e-mail boxes. No doubt about it. Technology has totally changed the way we manage time.

As for keeping in touch, it's estimated that at least twenty million people now carry beepers, an invention formerly the preserve of doctors who might be needed to help in a true crisis.

Paper

Our parents could not have imagined the amount of paper that now comes into our homes and offices. Whether it's junk mail or multiple copies of school notices, it's a deluge. Who has time to sort through it all?

Our Children

We love 'em, and do they take time! Running one's own schedule can be intense, but any parent will tell you that when you add in schedules for one, two, three, or more children, the experience becomes extremely time-consuming! What's more, the very nature of child rearing leads to a rush-rush atmosphere—hurrying to get a youngster out the door for school, rushing them along so they won't be late for an after-school class, even hurrying them to bed at night so they won't be too tired for all the rushing in store for them the next day.

And by the way, they're under stress, too. In addition to a normal homework load, many kids are shuttled from piano and karate to baseball practice and violin. The concept of a free afternoon is one that is long gone in this day and age.

Lack of Know-how

Some people don't understand how best to manage their time. Maybe they never learned to approach childhood tasks such as chores or homework in an organized fashion, or maybe life has just become too complex.

Without fundamental time-management skills, almost anyone living in the 1990s is going to be overwhelmed!

The World Around Us

Major businesses know we're rushed, and recent "improvements" on basic appliances have to do with cutting out waiting time. The latest toaster ovens toast faster than before, coffee makers brew more quickly, and many things are sold by appealing to us on a time basis. If we buy a Dustbuster, we don't have to waste time getting out a vacuum; we don't even have to take time to plug it in!

Unrealistic Expectations

People today are bombarded with opportunities never dreamed of in the past. Whether it's jetting across the country for a long weekend or aspiring to have a home that looks like a magazine cover, we want to be able to fit everything in (see it, do it, have it), and there just isn't enough time.

We also expect too much of ourselves—whether it's striving to be Superwoman or Dad of the Year and juggling home, work, and the expectations of others, or whether we're trying to "live life to its fullest" by packing in as much as we can every day, there comes a point when we have to say, "This isn't working."

It's long been known that successful people are those who take charge of their lives and:

- Set goals and make them happen

- Organize their time efficiently, so they can get things done without stress

- Balance work and personal lives for maximum results and satisfaction

- Remain motivated, beat procrastination, and get things done

In the past it still seemed manageable—if we just moved a little faster, did things a little quicker, organized a little better, we could still get it all done. But we soon found that while streamlining lots of the mundane tasks of life does save time (see Section 6, "Speed Tips and Shortcuts"), it isn't the only solution.

Today time management is also about learning new skills and learning about making choices. Time is finite, and there's no way to stretch it to fit in more than the hours allow.

For this reason, *The Overwhelmed Person's Guide to Time Management* is going to concentrate on three points:

1. It will help you focus on how you want to spend your time. By making hard decisions and setting priorities, you'll use the time available for what *you* want to do. You can relax because you know that you've selected what's most important to you and set aside enough time to devote to it—the ultimate in good time management.

2. It will provide you with the skills you need for good time management. The better the skills, the more time you'll have to devote to your top priorities. Time isn't flexible, but how you spend it is.

3. It will make you aware of the importance of scheduling leisure time and using it for leisure. This is actually an important principle of time management, for the person who takes a little time for him or herself actually returns feeling renewed and revived.

After reading this book you'll have a greater understanding of what you want to do with your time, and this knowledge will give you the control you need in order to find satisfaction and success.

Never again will you say: "I don't have the time." From now on you'll know that the time is there—waiting for you to choose how to spend it.

TEST YOUR TIME-MANAGEMENT SKILLS

When it comes to managing your time, what are your strengths and weaknesses? Take the following quiz to find out. For each question, check off the answer that best reflects your situation.

ALWAYS SOMETIMES NEVER

_____   _____   _____   1. Do you plan your day according to the daily "emergencies" of others?

_____   _____   _____   2. At the end of the day do you have lots of tasks left undone?

_____   _____   _____   3. Do you repeatedly run out of household necessities such as milk, juice, or ingredients for the next meal?

_____ _____ _____ 4. Are you frequently late to appointments?

_____ _____ _____ 5. Are you a procrastinator?

_____ _____ _____ 6. Do you frequently have to work late in the evening or early in the morning to make important deadlines?

_____ _____ _____ 7. If you need to locate a specific piece of paper (perhaps an invitation to a party or your latest credit card bill), would it take you more than five minutes to find it?

_____ _____ _____ 8. Do you forget friends' and relatives' birthdays more often than you would like to admit?

_____ _____ _____ 9. Is your desk frequently piled with papers?

_____ _____ _____ 10. Are you up to date on your filing?

_____ _____ _____ 11. Do you let the mail pile up?

_____ _____ _____ 12. Do you do tasks yourself because it's easier than teaching it to someone else?

_____ _____ _____ 13. Do you interrupt yourself by jumping up to do something else when you're working on a project?

_____ _____ _____ 14. Do you let other people waste your time with overly long telephone conversations or drop-by visits that never end?

_____ _____ _____ 15. Do you find that you're always losing things (from your keys to your glasses or library books)?

How to evaluate your scoring:

If you have fewer than 3 checks in the Always column:

You're doing quite well. (Wrap up this book and give it to a friend—the one who needs it the most.)

If you have 4–5 checks in the Always column:

You're well on your way to "overwhelmed," but not over the edge. If you go through this book, you'll learn enough good ideas that you'll be in control of your time in a flash.

If you have more than 5 checks in the Always column:

Life in the nineties has gotten the better of you, and you're *really* overwhelmed. I work with people like you all the time, and you'll identify with a lot of the stories in the book. Start reading. You'll soon find yourself less stressed and better organized.

CHAPTER 2

· · · · · · · ·

Just How Time Management Savvy Are You?

I work with people all the time who start out feeling that their situation is hopeless, that they'll never be able to better manage their time, that they are just too overwhelmed. Yet after talking, we're often able to isolate just one or two areas of difficulty. Yes, they are overwhelmed, but they are pleasantly surprised to learn that what seems to be a major stumbling block in their lives is really caused by only a single bad habit or two. This may be the case for you.

You may be terrific at some aspects of managing your time, but constantly getting tripped up by something that's becoming a way of life. Correcting this one tendency will set you on the road to better organization.

By learning what your particular "time-management style" is, you may come to a better understanding of what skills and systems are most valuable to you. Read through the following to see if you recognize yourself in any of these "time styles."

After starting a task, you become distracted—you notice a picture that needs straightening, or suddenly you remember a phone call you need to make, so you straighten the picture and then make the phone call. While on hold, you pull a file and decide to sort through it to pass the time. Fifteen minutes later, you still haven't made progress on the task you'd set out to do.

If this is you, then you're the *Self-Interrupter.* You may do well at other aspects of time management, but because you get distracted easily, it makes it difficult to accomplish major projects.

You're fun to be with. People peek in your office to say hello in the morning, and you not only greet them cheerfully, but you take a minute to tell about a hilarious phone call you got before leaving work last evening. And if someone's got a problem, you always have an empty chair where they can sit and talk until they feel better. In the meantime, the follow-up you were to do on your last assignment must wait; you have better things to do.

You're a great "people" person, but when it comes to getting tasks done—at home or at work, you're a *Time Waster.* If you learn to close your door now and then, you'll see that you can still get the work done, leaving plenty of other time for your personality to shine through.

■ ■ ■

You arrive . . . breathless. The doctor's, your mother's house, taking the children to school—you're never prompt. You're usually running behind (and someone somewhere is waiting for you), but even when you start out promptly, something always seems to come up.

If this is you, you already know that you're *Never on Time.* Wouldn't you like to get rid of that heart-pounding, palm-sweating habit of running late? You can do it by planning ahead.

■ ■ ■

"I gotta get off the phone! Something just happened!" "It's due tomorrow? I thought it was due Friday?" "I guess I'll pull an all-nighter on this one." Some people live their lives going from crisis to crisis. When do they file their taxes? April 15.

When do they do their Christmas shopping? Christmas eve. When do they pack for a trip? The night before, of course. Everything is an emergency, and pleasure is diminished because of the rush-rush atmosphere.

If this sounds familiar, you're a *Crisis Manager* who needs to learn to plan ahead so that you can feel in control of your time.

．．．

"I'll send you that contract," you say, and you do—but you send the wrong contract. Or the check goes out, but for the wrong amount. When it comes to the details, you're totally overwhelmed.

If this is you, call you *Scattered.* A little attention to managing the details, and you'll be fully in command of all that you do.

．．．

"I'll do it tomorrow." But of course, tomorrow never comes. Putting off doing something seems as though it will be easier than tackling the job at hand. "I'll have time next week to work on the report," you think. Next week comes and finds you suffering from a terrible cold. What do you do now?

If this sounds familiar, then you're the most famous of the infamous time managers, for you're the *Procrastinator.*

．．．

Got to pack for a trip, no problem. It's done. Got to get through the mail, no problem. You're done. Got to get through the grocery store, you're done in no time flat.

Label some people *Efficient.* What's missing? Nothing! Congratulations! Keep doing what you're doing.

．．．

"I don't know whether to answer the phone or finish the letter . . . do the filing or make the airline reservations . . ." Setting moment-to-moment priorities can be very difficult, particularly when your priorities are partly being performed for someone else. The boss says everything is a crisis or emergency, and you're left going in circles.

Many people I see are simply *Undirected*. They haven't thought through their priorities, so they don't know where to begin. As a result of their indecision, they also worry. It takes them a long time to make an initial decision, and then once it's made, the Undirected wastes more time second-guessing that decision!

■ ■ ■

Need another committee person for the fund-raiser? Need an extra hand to help on the report? Want to discuss the interesting article you just read in *The New Yorker*? Call *The Juggler*. This type of person is adept at managing an innumerable number of tasks, and they even make it look easy! Priorities seem to fall into place, and they work quickly and get an enormous amount done. While Jugglers do sometimes pay a price (and *no* is a vocabulary word they need to be reminded of), they are to be credited for their ability to see straight and keep things under control.

■ ■ ■

This type of person drives everyone else crazy. Everyone is still sitting at dinner, and yet one family member is already neatening up—scraping the plates at the end of the table, wiping the butter off the edge of a knife, doing all that he or she can to bring order instantly, despite the enjoyable family conversation taking place. At the office, this person can't stand it if a mistake is made or if some information for a report is held up for a day. Absolutely everything needs to be done correctly and on time!

While organization and excellence are worthy goals, the *Obsessively Organized* can't let one piece of paper or one dish sit there, and they focus on organization for organization's sake, not for what's truly important. This behavior makes those around them nervous to the point that it hurts the overall functioning of any group. Sometimes being a good time manager means knowing when to ease up on others so that they can feel comfortable enough to do their best.

■ ■ ■

Did you find yourself? If so, your Time Style will help you know what to work on first. Throughout the book are solutions to all the obstacles encountered by these various personalities. For instance, if you are a Self-Interrupter, you'll want to be sure to read Chapter 6, "How to Manage the Time You Have," Chapter 8, "Getting It Done!," Chapter 17, "Interruptions," and Chapter 18, "The Two P's." Never on Time should turn to Chapter 10, "Getting There on Time," and Chapter 11, "Time-Management Emergencies." And there's even reading for Efficient, who has likely already read Chapter 23, "170 Ways to Do Things Better."

If you want to get started on breaking one particular bad habit first, scan the table of contents. It will lead you to the chapters most relevant to you. Then you can attack the rest of the book.

It's time to take that first step toward better time management. Let's get started!

CHAPTER 3

. . . .

The Importance of Systems

Systems are one of the most important elements of good time management. Think how we struggle when an activity is unfamiliar or we don't have a routine way of doing something—from locating your toothbrush the first night in a hotel to starting a new job.

By definition a system is a routine way of getting something done. Systems save time by allowing you to do things automatically. Our lives run more smoothly when we use systems to take care of the details, leaving us more energy for the demands and events that are part of "real life."

Getting through the mail daily is a great example of a system that will help you manage your time. (Chapter 14 explains how to create an efficient system for your mail.) If you handle it regularly—and get through all of it every day—you'll save yourself time, reduce household or office paper clutter, and be in control of all the information that has been sent to you.

Because systems are such an important part of time management, this chapter will examine creating systems when there aren't any, and it will introduce you to a vital tool for time management: a master notebook. We'll discuss:

- Creating systems

  1. Systems for physical possessions
  2. Mutually agreed-upon systems
  3. Systems for taking care of the routine

- Your master notebook

Systems for Physical Possessions

Physical possessions are so easy to manage if you have a system, so difficult if you don't: bills, the mail, filing, a child's outgrown clothing you're saving for a sibling, holiday decorations—the list could go on and on.

Look around your home or office. Are there areas that just don't work for you—whenever you need something, does it take extra time? Consider what kind of system might help. While many answers are found in this book, it's also important to develop the skills of creating a system for whatever comes up.

Here are some typical areas where people run into trouble managing physical possessions.

- Is it difficult to find what you've got stashed in the attic? Take adhesive-backed labels or index cards (lined ones are convenient for listing contents), tape, and a pen to the attic, check the contents of each box, and attach a label.

- Always misplacing library books? Establish a specific place to keep them. And if you're constantly forgetting the due date, that system is easy: When you get home from the library, make a note of the due date in your calendar. (Teach your children to do the same.)

- Are you forever groping for the spices you need when you cook? Purchase a lazy Susan or a spice rack, and place the spice bottles in alphabetical order.

- At the office you may find that people are constantly leaving memos in the middle of your desk, on top of ongoing work. Set up a well-labeled In box and ask that they use it. That way you can go through the new papers at a time that's convenient for you.

- If you're staying in a hotel room for more than one night, it's worth setting up a system. Unpack and put your clothing in drawers (just as you would place them at home) so that you don't have to burrow through your suitcase for what you're going to wear each day. Finding what you need will be automatic since you've duplicated your "at home" storage system as closely as possible.

Mutually Agreed-upon Systems

When others are involved, it's important to work out mutually agreed-upon systems to save time. Some systems are longstanding: If everyone at the office agrees to notify the supply department as soon as someone opens the last container of copy toner, your department won't ever be caught short. The same methodology will work with the family grocery list.

Other systems must be planned for each occasion. Where will you meet your spouse for dinner? How is your son getting to and from school after soccer practice? You have to agree on a plan.

Have you and your kids or you and your spouse ever worked out a "secret" system? If the event you're all attending is boring and someone wants to leave, you establish a code word that, within the family, means, "Lets get out of here!" Systems work!

Systems for Taking Care of the Routine

For every mundane task there should be a system. The routine nature of it removes:

- Any emotion about the event. Instead of thinking, "Oh, I hate paying bills and don't want to do it," you'll find yourself saying: "It's the first of the month, better pay those bills."

- Any thought of not doing it. If you *always* change the beds or do the grocery shopping on a certain day, you'll find the routine of it makes it easy to do instead of thinking about when else you could possibly fit it in.

Systems are usually easy to create. You need to evaluate:

1. What needs to be accomplished?
2. Does it need to be done in a specific order?
3. Do I need any specific tools or equipment for getting it done?

Then you need to establish a schedule. This is key. By scheduling time for a task, you'll find it much easier to get it done.

Systems require time to create and long-term repetition and discipline to maintain, but the savings in time and in stress make the investment well worth the effort.

Your Master Notebook: Your First System for Time (and Paper) Management

A master notebook is a key system for creating an organized life, for it provides *one place* for listing all that you have to do— both long-term and short-term.

Your master notebook is your long-term planner and the perfect supplement to your calendar/day planner. I generally recommend that clients keep their personal master notebook at home and a work-related one at the office.

Here's what you need to do to create your notebook:

- Purchase a spiral notebook or a small (6.5 by 9) loose-leaf. I recommend this medium-size notebook because it will be big enough to hold all you need, yet still small enough to be portable when you want it to be.

- If you choose to use the loose-leaf system, you'll also need a supply of paper and subject dividers.

- Assemble your notebook and create headings for the categories that are applicable to your life. You may want to organize your notebook by task: "To Do," "To Buy," or "To Call." Subject headings sometimes work better: "House," "Family," "Vacation," "Volunteer Projects." You may need to create a new category for something that's important to you for a temporary period of time such as "Kitchen Renovation" or "Hospital Fund-raiser." Note: If you prefer to use a spiral notebook, you can't create categories the way you can with a loose-leaf. Instead, your entries will be chronological and will serve as a running log of information.

- Now gather together all your scraps and lists to combine them into one master list in your notebook. As you recopy the tasks, assign them to various pages according to the appropriate heading.

At home and at the office your master notebook serves as a diary, a confirmation, and a permanent reminder of ideas, information, and even telephone conversations.

- All tasks should be written down with the date on which you entered the listing. When you look back through the notebook, the dating will provide you with a method of assessing how long something has been pending. It will also provide verification of phone calls. When you call a store to ask why you have not yet received your merchandise, you'll have a record that you've spoken to them about this matter on three previous occasions.

- Break major tasks into small steps and write them down. "Plan vacation" sounds fun but overwhelming. However, steps make it manageable. Your notations might look like this:

- Plan vacation

  - Check school calendar!

  - Select dates that work for whole family.

  - Call Martha for the name of the hotel where she stayed last year.

  - Check with travel agent re: possible discounts.

  - Pick up guidebooks at bookstore.

- To keep your notebook up to date, remove pages on which all items have been crossed off. Keep these pages in a file (or save the old spiral notebooks, if you're using that system) for at least a year. If you haven't needed to refer back to them in that time, you probably won't need to.

The beauty of the notebook system is that you aren't limited by space constraints. If you have a great opening line for a speech you need to give in a couple of months, you can take a separate page in your office master notebook and note down the line and some thoughts about the speech. As the date nears, create a file for your notes and transfer the page to the file at that time. What most people would have written on a scrap of paper and mislaid in a "to file" pile, you'll have easily accessible in your master notebook!

TOO MANY CARRY-OVER ITEMS?

When your master notebook becomes overwhelmed by tasks that just aren't getting done, go back through the list, item by item. Consider:

- Does this really need to be done?

- Could I delegate this or hire someone else to do it?

- Place carry-over items that you deem important in order of priority. Schedule in as many as you can and work through the list, making certain that this time each one of the tasks gets done.

Checkpoint and Review

1. Good systems take care of life's details, saving your energy for more important matters. Therefore, it's important to:

- Establish systems for storing or organizing physical possessions.

- Work out mutually acceptable systems with others, anything from where to meet on a given day to setting up an ongoing system so all family members can help keep track of needed groceries.

- Create systems for as many of life's routine tasks as you can.

2. Create a master notebook for ongoing to-do items.
Purchase a medium-size loose-leaf or spiral notebook.

- If you buy a loose-leaf, use tabbed dividers and label them according to the categories that are important to your life.

- Write down and date everything that comes to mind. This will provide a running list of all that you need to do, and from this list it will be easy to create a daily to-do list.

Section 2

People, Places, and Things to Do

books can do so much more than keep track of dates. There is plenty of room to note appointments and business expenses. Address books are bound in with the planners, and space is provided for to-do lists where we can set goals, coordinate projects, and keep track of ideas.

When you consider the additional option of switching to a computerized planner or a hand-held organizer, you'll see that choosing a planner has become as complex as the rest of our lives. So what will it be? Paper? Computer? Or a hand-held electronic system (often called a "personal digital assistant" or "palm-top computer")?

This chapter will present you with some pros and cons to consider in selecting from among the following:

- A paper-based planner

- Planner software for your personal computer

- A handheld electronic planner or palm-top computer

You'll also learn what you need to about:

- family calendars

- address books

Paper-Based Daily Planners

Despite the amazing features that the latest computerized planners offer, there is still a lot to be said for paper-based planners. One of my clients who owns his own small business says it best:

"I carried a laptop computer with me for two years, and I liked the software scheduling system I used, but it was still more trouble than a paper-based calendar. Every time I wanted to enter something, I had to turn on the system. With paper I just flip open my book."

CHAPTER 4

· · · · · · · ·

Keeping Track of Places to Be and People to Call: Your Daily Planner and Address Book

Whenever clients mention that they have trouble with appointments or scheduling, I always ask how many planners they keep. Invariably, they admit to keeping more than one. They'll have a calendar at home and one at work, or one on the computer and a desk calendar as well.

Any system involving more than one calendar or planner creates additional complications. You may have entered a breakfast meeting on the calendar at the office, but if you've forgotten to write it down at home, chances are you'll miss your breakfast appointment. Maintaining more than one daily planner becomes confusing because it's difficult to coordinate all the scheduling.

While it's preferable to maintain just one calendar system, there is one exception. If you're trying to coordinate family activities, then you'll need a family calendar in addition to your own daily planner. The benefits of the entire family being able to view what's ahead outweigh the negatives of having to cross-check everything. See below for more information.

Note, too, my choice of terms. Today the term *daily planner* is far more appropriate than *calendar*. Today's scheduling

For people who are near a computer all day or those who are intrigued by the gadgetry of the new palm-top computer, the new systems may open up a wonderful new world, but for most a paper-based system is still more than adequate.

One woman pointed out an aesthetic reason: "I like having a planning book. Every year I look for one that is practical but interesting. One year I used one that offered interesting recipes; this year the book I'm using has great fashion photos. It takes the drudgery out of scheduling!"

THE ADVANTAGES OF A PAPER-BASED PLANNER

- They are portable.

- They are always accessible.

- You don't have to turn it on in order to access the information.

- There's no initial time investment to enter information.

- Data can't be destroyed through an electronic breakdown.

- Your planner is valuable only to you; no one would bother to steal it.

- They are the least expensive type of calendar/planning system.

- They are a comfortable, handy tool of time management.

DISADVANTAGES

- Paper-based systems lack some of the time-saving "bells and whistles" that computer planners have.

- Each year you need to transfer important dates such as birthdays and anniversaries; with computer planners this is done electronically.

Selecting a Paper-Based System

Talk to other people about what planners they use and visit stores to see and compare what is available. You are primarily looking for one that:

- Is easy to carry, factoring in your lifestyle

- Has ample space for each day's appointments

- Provides room for a daily to-do list on the same page as your appointment schedule

- Has a part of the calendar that lets you see several months in advance

- Has an attachment that holds your pen

Computer Planners

Calendar/planners on computer are great organizers and usually combine an appointment book, address book, to-do list, and space for other types of notations. Well-designed versions of these systems can be relatively easy to use, and the time-management possibilities are amazing.

ADVANTAGES TO A COMPUTER PLANNER

- Easy rescheduling. With a few key strokes, a canceled meeting on Tuesday can be moved to Friday, complete with data on location, telephone number, and driving directions.

- Scheduling availability at a glance. If someone calls you to set up an appointment, click on the appropriate icon (symbol) and you'll get a view of your week. Times at which you're already booked show up in black; your available meeting times are shown in white.

- Dual or group scheduling. In an office, a secretary and boss can both input into the same system, making it easy to coordinate schedules and stay up to date. Group scheduling can also be accomplished for workers on a local area network system; a meeting can be entered into everyone's personal planner (though parts of your schedule are "public" through the system, parts can be kept private, too).

- Recurring appointments (a monthly orthodontic appointment for your teen, for example) can be set to appear automatically.

- Auto-dial and auto-fax on computers with a modem hookup. If you want to fax a letter to a contact, you simply look up the contact's name and fax number in your address book, highlight the letter you've written, and hit the fax icon on the software, which automatically sends the letter to your contact. To follow up by phone, click on the phone icon in the address book, and you'll speak directly to your contact.

- To-do list carry-over features. "Buy film" will keep reappearing on your list until you've actually taken care of the matter.

- Time summary analyses

- Search capabilities. The computer will help you identify the date of your next dental appointment.

- Space for logs of phone calls and notes. The latest versions feature "contact manager" functions where notes can be made about a phone conversation you had with someone, and when you want to recall what was said, you can pull up the person's name and find a recap of the conversation.

DISADVANTAGES

- Lacks portability (unless you carry a computer notebook regularly). You must create a paper printout to carry with you, bringing you back to a paper-based calendar system.

- A computer crash or disk error can wipe you out. If you choose this system, *back up frequently!*

Shopping for a Computer-Based System

If you opt for a computer calendar system, you'll choose between:

1. A family-oriented program (which usually features calendar, address book, and to-do list) that is easy enough for a child to use but designed to manage the time of an entire family
2. A personal home office–style program with many more features (such as cross-referencing and communications features) that is meant for adult use only

At your computer store ask to see a family organizer or a personal organizer program. There are many brands available, and only you can decide what will work for you or your family.

- Talk to friends as well as asking for in-store demonstrations.

- Look for something basic and easy to use. Even the simplest systems have most of the above capabilities. Many of the advanced features are necessary only for office workers looking for the group-scheduling features. Make a list (put it in your master notebook) of the features that are important to you, and then see how well each competitive system manages those features.

Hand-held Electronic Planners

This category of calendar requires some terminology clarification. At this time an *electronic organizer* or a *personal information manager* is a hand-held computer with limited uses. They are designed to keep phone lists, addresses, and appointments, but the information generally cannot be fed into your computer.

A *personal digital assistant* is a hand-held computer (now referred to as a "palm-top" computer) that usually adheres to PC standards and can interface with other technology (you can connect it to a fax machine, an online service, or exchange data between your personal computer and your hand-held unit). These function like an organizer, keeping track of phone numbers and appointments. They often include word processing and spread sheet capabilities and sometimes offer wireless communications (faxing and data reception), and handwriting recognition (so that notations can be made in handwriting rather than by keyboarding).

Eventually these two distinctions will probably become obsolete, and all hand-held electronic planners will function as personal digital assistants, but for the time being, consumers must ask the right questions to be certain that the unit you purchase has the capabilities you need.

ADVANTAGES OF A PERSONAL DIGITAL ASSISTANT

- A terrific system for keeping track of your life electronically.

- Portable. When purchasing, evaluate weight. Some models are heavier than others.

- Notes taken while at an out-of-office meeting can be entered into your computer via the system.

DISADVANTAGES

- Costly, though prices will continue to drop.

- Possibility of poor design. Some are not well thought out for ease of use and best manipulation.

- They occasionally freeze up. While improvements are happening constantly, most longtime users have their "crash" stories.

Shopping for a Personal Digital Assistant

- How is the system powered, and how long will it last?

- Can you download to and from other machines?

- Is there protection against a crash in which you would lose all your data?

- If you're selecting a keyboard system, is it comfortable for your hand size? Some keyboards are very small, and consumers report difficulty in using them.

- Check out the screen display. Some screens are difficult to read in certain light. Shop for one that is "backlit," and check it out in various types of lighting.

- If you're interested in a pen-based system, test it. Can it read *your* handwriting? Check for accuracy.

General Planner Tips

Keep your planner open and available so that you are constantly aware of your schedule. Many who use a computer planner create daily printouts for this purpose.

When you set up an appointment, note the address, telephone number, and directions in the space next to the appointment. That way you'll have all the information you need when you need it.

Review your activities a week in advance so that you can plan around your existing appointments. If you have a dental appointment in a particular neighborhood, you may want to schedule an appointment with a client who is also in that area.

Make appointments with yourself to be certain you have time for your priorities. (See Chapter 6.)

Couples should set aside a few minutes weekly to review upcoming plans and compare schedules. That way you've both noted in your own calendars any plans that involve you as a couple. Also note your spouse's plans if they affect your own schedule. (If one of you works late one night, the other might like to join a friend at the movies.)

If you need to coordinate your schedule with a boss, secretary, or co-worker, establish a weekly meeting time when you compare schedules and review the week ahead.

Check your planner every day! You'd be surprised at how many people don't.

The Family Calendar

Select a large wall calendar (17″ × 22″ is a good size) so that there is space for complete notations about activities. Hang the calendar in a central location near a telephone so that when calls regarding scheduling come in, you can easily check the calendar.

Purchase colored pens and assign a color to each member of the family. (Select a separate color for activities that involve everyone.) All notations pertaining to that person should be made in the appropriate color. Place a pencil holder nearby for storing the markers, or put them in an easily accessible drawer.

Go through school calendars as well as after-school, sports, and religious schedules and note all significant dates. That way you'll know that all activities and events for the year (or the season) are already reflected on the calendar.

Teach children (age eight and older) to take responsibility for their own scheduling, noting birthday parties, play dates, and special events they want to attend. They'll quickly learn that if they want to go, they must write it down.

Of course, vital to making a family calendar work is coordinating it with your personal calendar:

- Check the calendar nightly to be certain that nothing new has been added by another family member. If something has and it will affect you, note it on your personal planner.

■ If you make plans at work that affect the family, note it on the family calendar when you get home.

Your Personal Address Book

If you're satisfied with your current address book, that's surprising. In today's world, we all come with so many "address" tags that most books lack enough space for each listing. For example, here is just some of the information you might like to write down about someone:

Name
Address
Home telephone
Office telephone
Fax number (possibly for home and office)
E-mail address
Beeper number
Cellular or car phone

And that's a minimum of information! With many contacts, you may want both a home and business address, as well as space for some personal information such as spouse's and children's names or birth dates.

One possible solution is a "roll file" where all names, telephone numbers, and addresses are kept on cards that can be easily snapped in and out. These are simple to update (just create a new card and toss out the old one), and the cards themselves provide adequate space for all the information you would like to note down about that person. (You can save time by attaching a business card to one of the roll-file cards and writing out any additional information you may need.)

The one big drawback to this system is portability. If you need to carry your address book, this is not the system for you.

Instead, you might prefer a computer solution. If you have not opted for a palm-top computer that will provide you with a portable address book, consider entering your information on your personal computer and creating a printout of the computerized address book. Current planner computer programs provide ample space for the information you'll want, and the information is easy to update. A printout placed in a binder provides you with the advantages of a paper copy (so that you avoid constantly turning on your computer for an address or phone number). Information changes are also easy to execute with this system: Enter the necessary changes and print out a new page to insert into your address book. You'll always have a clean, up-to-date book with a minimum of work.

There are several extra advantages to a computerized address book:

- Each entry can be assigned a category. You may not remember the name of the person who repairs your computer, but by asking for a search of the "computer repair" category, it will pull up anyone to whom you've assigned that designation. Categories are limitless, from "accountants" to "window washers."

- You can conduct a contact search by location. If you're going to be in Denver on business, you can pull up all your contacts in that area—a task that will take only seconds by computer and would be time consuming to do by hand.

- If your modem and computer lines are integrated, you can click on a telephone number in the directory, and the computer will dial the number for you.

- Because a new copy is as easy as pressing "print," you needn't suffer with messy, marked-up pages that make note of all recent address changes.

- If you should ever lose your loose-leaf address notebook, you have an instant backup on the computer.

The biggest drawback to a computer system is the time it takes to enter the names, addresses, and phone numbers.

(Some systems allow you to transfer any information you already have in your computer so that you needn't reenter it.) The best way to do the job is by assigning yourself the task of entering a dozen names a day. You can easily accomplish this task in five to ten minutes, and over a period of a few weeks the entire job will get done.

Get in the habit of updating the computer data whenever you receive a change-of-address notification. You can change your binder copy by hand or print out a new page.

If you don't have a computer, don't want to bother computerizing all the names, or are unsuccessful at finding a telephone directory with enough space, consider creating your own using a small notebook with dividers where you can write expanded entries when necessary. (If you use this system, photocopy the pages so that you'll have a backup in case it's lost.)

Checkpoint and Review

1. Investigate paper-based, computer software, and hand-held electronic planners and select the one that best suits your lifestyle. Keep in mind:

- Convenience

- Portability

- Cost

- Ease of coordination with spouse, family, or staff members

- Special features you think you would use

2. Use your planner intelligently.

- Keep it available at all times.

- Make complete notations (address and telephone number along with appointments).

- Review weekly and coordinate with family members or staff.

- Be sure to check it every day!

3. Establish a family calendar.

- Use different-colored markers for different family members.

- Make certain that you coordinate your personal appointments with family dates.

4. Select an address book with ample space for entries. Choose from:

- A roll-file system

- A computer-based system with paper copy

- Make your own using a notebook and dividers

- Keep your address book up to date, adding new information as it comes in

CHAPTER 5

. . . .

Keeping Track of What You Need to Do: Your "To Do" List

Overwhelmed by scraps of paper? Most people are: Here's how it happens:

- The person on the phone asks that you drop something in the mail to them, so you make a note of it—on the back of an envelope.

- You're in the kitchen and you think of a great gift idea for a friend, so you write it down—on a scrap torn from a Chinese menu.

- A neighbor happens to mention a great tile layer for the new kitchen floor you plan, so you take the information—writing it on a paper napkin.

- You've come back from a business luncheon with two new phone numbers, one on a business card (but you can't remember which person gave you the card), and the other on a matchbook cover (and you don't even smoke).

At the office it's almost the same. These notes and reminders may be written on a page from an adhesive-backed notepad, a piece of scrap paper, or the back of a letter. No matter how well it's written, it's not organized. What you're left with is lots of little pieces of paper—*if* you can put your hands on them!

Some of my clients do a little better. They've read the importance of a to-do list, and they have them—yes, more than one: a list for work, a list for home, a list of things to pack for vacation, a list of errands for the weekend. One client had so many lists he had to keep lists of his lists!

None of these methods work. It's too hard to locate the scraps of paper or the multiple lists when you need them. Where *is* that Saturday errand list when you think of an additional thing to do?

Having a single, useful to-do list will be one of your most important tools of time management. You maintain control of your life by keeping track of what's important to you, and you maintain control of your time by scheduling these activities in order of priority and according to time available. You've set a schedule for getting things done.

> ***Writing it down means you don't
> have to worry about forgetting it.***

This chapter will show you how to:

- Plan your list for the week.

- Update nightly.

- Work with a computerized to-do list.

Planning Your To-Do List for the Week

General planning should be done weekly and involves working with both your planner and your master notebook.

Most people do it on Sunday night (or work-related tasks might be planned on Friday afternoon before leaving the office).

This is your opportunity to take a general look at the week and come to an understanding of what is possible and what isn't. If you have many appointments and an all-day conference one week, this is likely not the time to start a new long-range project. However, if it's a priority item, make a note in your daily planner for the following Monday that you must start then—otherwise these things can slip.

- Your daily to-do list should be written in your calendar/planner.

- Review your calendar for the upcoming week, examining it for two things:

  - Do any of your appointments take you to neighborhoods where you can easily do another task from your to-do list? An appointment at the ophthalmologist might take you right past a store your mother loves. With her birthday coming up, this may be the perfect time to stop in and see if they have something you'd like to give her.

  - Review your appointments for the upcoming week. Do you need to make special preparations for any of them, and do you need to write these items on your to-do list? If you're not yet finished with a report needed for one of your business appointments, that task will then become a priority. Or if this is your week to bring a snack to the Little League game, you'd better add the items you'll need to your grocery list.

- After considering any extra blocks of time you have available, comb through your master notebook. What tasks could you take care of during those blocks of time? Write them down.

- *Don't* overschedule. Write down what you conservatively feel you will be able to accomplish. That way you won't feel overwhelmed, and you will have a feeling of accomplishment at being able to do what you set out to do for the day.

The Nightly Update

This weekly planning session gives you a general idea of what the week holds. On a nightly basis you need to update the plan for the next day:

- You may discover that an unexpected emergency prevented you from accomplishing the tasks you intended to do one day, so those items must be moved forward to another day.

- An appointment may be cancelled, providing you with the perfect block of time to finish something old or start something new.

- Your boss has requested something, adding a new priority to your week. You need to juggle your day to accommodate this.

- As you complete tasks, they should be crossed off your master notebook list and your daily planner list.

THE COMPUTERIZED TO-DO LIST

Like the computerized daily planner, there is a lot to be said for the to-do list on computer:

What's wonderful:

- Lets you keep a running record of things you need to do without ever recopying

- Integrates the to-do list with your appointment calendar

- Sorts tasks by priority, category, status, or start date

- Family organizer programs create to-do lists for various family members

What's not so wonderful:

- If your lifestyle doesn't involve being near a computer, the negatives may outweigh the benefits right now.

If you've opted for a hand-held personal digital assistant or have a laptop computer that you carry with you, you may find that you have the best of both worlds: a computerized method of maintaining a to-do list with an easily accessible piece of electronic gear.

Checkpoint and Review

Build your daily to-do list from your master notebook.

- Do general planning weekly.

- Update your list nightly so that you can make any necessary adjustments.

- Don't overschedule.

Section 3

GETTING IT DONE . . .
AND ON TIME

CHAPTER 6

· · · · · · · · ·

How to Manage the Time You Have: Planning and Priorities

How Overwhelmed Are You?

- You wake up at seven a.m., and you have that sinking feeling: "I still have twelve things to do that I should have done yesterday!"
- The phone doesn't stop ringing.
- The kids have interrupted you eight times in ten minutes.
- The washing machine is on the blink.
- The repairman hasn't shown up.
- The asphalt company "forgets" to send someone back to do the final phase of your driveway.
- The entire family's been sick with a cold for a week, and now you have it.
- The repairman hasn't shown up.
- The report has to be on your boss's desk the day after tomorrow.
- You've got an appointment and you've left yourself only ten minutes to get there; the problem is it's fifteen minutes away.

- It's your night to volunteer at the community food-distribution program.
- The cleaners lost your favorite suit.
- The repairman hasn't shown up.

At times like this it feels like the world is closing in on you. Who has time to plan or set priorities when there are so many interruptions and daily emergencies that come up?

Most of our days are spent just keeping up with what we perceive are the have-to-do tasks of daily life. At home we get bogged down by a ringing telephone, a washing machine that overflows and has to be replaced, or an emergency errand like getting to the cleaners with a suit you need for the next day. If we have kids, then our day may begin with the realization that everything planned must be unplanned; Jeremy has the chicken pox.

At work, it's the minutiae: reading the mail, handling phone calls, attending meetings, answering requests from your boss or other departments. In our culture, "thinking" doesn't look or feel like work, so it tends to be scheduled for "when you have time." Of course, that time rarely comes.

We do think ahead on some things. We'll "plan" a vacation, or decide on a specific movie to see on Saturday night, but we rarely give much thought to mapping out what we'd like our life to look like in a month, a year, or five years from now. Without making conscious choices about how we use our time (and creating that map in the process), there's no way to achieve what you really intend to in life.

This chapter will help you start creating that map by showing you how to identify your goals. With careful planning you will gain control over the personal direction you want your life to take, and you'll soon see that the most outrageous dream can become a goal that can be achieved—one step at a time. First, we'll examine dreams vs. goals, and then we'll follow a six-step route to getting on track for the life for which *you* want to have time:

1. Setting goals
2. Establishing priorities
3. Evaluating where your time goes
4. Cutting back on old "time habits"
5. Simplifying your life
6. Learning to say no

The Difference Between a Dream and a Goal

Some people have dreams; wiser people have goals. I've spoken to many mothers, temporarily at home with their children, who have long-range dreams. Many intend to go back to school or start their own business, but when you ask about what kind of additional education they want or how they'll finance their new business, the conversation gets fuzzy, and soon we're back to talking about how best to cope with separation anxiety. Men aren't immune to this pattern, either. Many tell me of entrepreneurial dreams they intend to pursue on retirement, but they haven't a clue as to what they really need to do first.

Dreams are idealized pictures with no pathways for getting from here to there. Goals often consist of the same ideal, but they also have a logical set of steps to make that dream a reality.

DREAMS	GOALS
Picture of happy family having dinner together	To reorganize schedules so that the family eats together at least three nights per week
Working from home doing something	To start a college-counseling business for high school students
To look great in a bathing suit	To follow a sensible weight loss program and incorporate an exercise plan three to four times per week

Goals have an action plan. They provide a decision-making framework that will help in every aspect of your life. If you have goals, instead of feeling overwhelmed when too many demands are placed on you, you'll be able to say: "Does this fit in with what I want out of life?" If it does, you'll know to place it among your priorities.

If it doesn't, you can make an educated choice. "This task does not fit with my priorities, but it is something I need to do anyway." We all have to do some tasks in life that we would prefer not to (donating cookies for your child's classroom bake sale; returning a sweater to a department store; rewriting something for work), but other tasks are an easy no if we realize that they don't fit in with our long-term plans (to volunteer your services—again; to sit through a seminar given by someone whom you've heard speak before).

With a little effort we can make some changes to create time for the want-to-do's—our own priorities. Here's how to start.

Time for What?

What would you like to do that you don't have time for now? If you make the time, dreams really can come true!

What do you want more of in your life? Time for yourself? Time for family? Time for starting your own business? Time to get an additional degree or professional accreditation? Start this process by creating a vision of your ideal.

Recognize that there are certain things you really like to do that are sometimes forgotten in the confusion of daily life. You may love playing tennis, but because of job and family demands, you've quit setting aside time for an activity that you find to be great fun and great exercise. Or you may have always intended to travel to Africa, but you've just never investigated how to come up with the time or the money so you can do it.

How often has the wish list of things you'd like to have time for gone up in smoke? As an exercise, think back over the past year and fill in the blank: "I wish I'd spent more time_____

_____

_____."

Step 1. Set Goals and Write Them Down

The goals you establish should be written down—it's a good way to promise yourself you'll keep them.

Take three pieces of paper, or use the work pages provided (see next page). On the first, write down what you would like to be doing in ten years (working in a different field? have children? retire?). Take several days to consider what you want your future to hold, and then settle on the one or two long-range plans on which you'd like to focus.

Record on the second sheet what you would like to be doing in two years. Perhaps you'd like a promotion at work or to be spending more time on a specific hobby. Or if your long-range goal requires advanced education (such as going to business school or getting a Ph.D.), then on this sheet of paper you should note down what you would need to be doing during the next two years to accomplish these long-range goals.

In ten years I would like to:

Write what you see yourself doing and note down the goals you would like to have achieved.

In two years I would like to:

Write what you see yourself doing and note down the goals you would like to have achieved.

My short-term (six-month) goals are:

Some of these goals will need to be steps on the way to achieving your longer-term goals.

Short-term goals belong on your third sheet of paper. If you have to apply to graduate schools as part of your long-range plan, then a short-term goal would include taking the entrance exams.

Research may be required before you can move ahead with a goal. If you don't know what is necessary to become a licensed physical therapist, then you will need to investigate the requirements before knowing what steps you need to take to prepare.

Other short-term goals might include starting an exercise program or learning a new skill—just for fun.

As you note your goals, be specific. If your goal is to learn a new language for a trip abroad, do you want to speak like a native, or learn enough phrases to get by? The more specific you are, the easier it will be to act on your goals.

Don't try to accomplish the impossible. If you work full-time, enrolling in two night courses in a new field may be unrealistic; start with one class so that the goals you set are achievable.

Keep your goal sheets nearby so that you can refer to them regularly. (Your master notebook is an ideal spot.)

Step 2. Establishing Priorities

Review your goal sheets weekly, selecting a reasonable number of tasks to undertake during the upcoming week. Realize that you can do anything you want, but you can't do *everything*, so be selective.

Plan how you will make your goals manageable by breaking each one into small steps. If one of your short-term goals is losing weight, then you'll want to note steps such as visiting your doctor, selecting a diet plan, and starting a new exercise program. A longer-term goal such as moving to a new community would involve sending for literature, researching the job market, contacting realtors, investigating schools (if you have children), etc.

Set priorities so that you can focus on the most important tasks first. Otherwise, you might invest your energy on insignificant matters instead of what's most productive.

Set realistic deadlines for various steps on the way to your goals. A goal without a deadline can become nothing more than an unfulfilled New Year's resolution. There's something about a date that makes a plan very real. If you want to join a health club and haven't investigated them yet, set a deadline (write it in your notebook and in your daily planner) for having called or visited three or four.

Plan to reward yourself for meeting deadlines. Mini-rewards (a new paperback book? meeting a friend at your favorite coffee bar?) for achieving several small steps along the way can provide a nice boost for work well done.

Stay on track. Sometimes circumstances prevent us from following our own priorities. (Your child is sick, and you have to reduce your work week, or the boss has required extensive overtime, meaning that you've missed some of your night classes.) When you've had to tend to other matters, just do what you can to get back to your priorities as soon as possible.

For a reminder about setting daily priorities and working from a to-do list, refer back to Chapter 5.

Step 3. Evaluating Where Your Time Goes

Refer to the following time chart. Make copies of this one or design a time chart that reflects your schedule. You'll need to keep track of your time for at least a week (carry the chart with you; tuck it in your planner or put it in your master notebook), and I recommend sporadic "time" check-ups long after that. It's important that you chart your time for weekends as well as weekdays. Many of my personal clients say, "I just don't know where the weekends go!"

The chart enables you to account for all aspects of your day, from morning grooming and commuting time to how long it takes to fix dinner. (Once you're in the habit, it will take only a few minutes to fill in.) You'll be surprised at how much time grooming, errands, and around-town transportation takes!

It's important to examine exactly how much time is under your control:

DAILY TIME CHART

6:00 A.M.	10:30
6:15	10:45
6:30	11:00
6:45	11:15
7:00	11:30
7:15	11:45
7:30	12:00 NOON
7:45	12:15
8:00	12:30
8:15	12:45
8:30	1:00
8:45	1:15
9:00	1:30
9:15	1:45
9:30	2:00
9:45	2:15
10:00	2:30
10:15	2:45

DAILY TIME CHART (cont'd)

3:00	7:45
3:15	8:00
3:30	8:15
3:45	8:30
4:00	8:45
4:15	9:00
4:30	9:15
4:45	9:30
5:00	9:45
5:15	10:00
5:30	10:15
5:45	10:30
6:00	10:45
6:15	11:00
6:30	11:15
6:45	11:30
7:00	11:45
7:15	12:00 MIDNIGHT
7:30	

Some people like to highlight their time chart with colors in order to better visualize distribution of time. Select colors for the following categories:

- Office

- Home-related tasks such as errands and chores

- Personal/family time

As you study your time sheets, you will likely be surprised at how long you spend on certain activities. And you may be surprised at the number of times you were obviously interrupted. Look for patterns (did you interrupt yourself? did someone else interrupt you?), so you can begin changing those behaviors. (See Chapter 17 for more information on handling interruptions.)

Step 4. Dropping Old Habits and Activities

Next, use your completed time charts to begin evaluating what's making you feel overwhelmed. What do you want less of? Fewer late nights at the office? Less time spent on household drudgery? Fewer interruptions during the time you do give yourself?

Assess today's priorities. At home, what is most important to you? Spending time with a spouse? Being with your children? Reading? Working on a hobby? Look at your time charts: How successful are you at making time for those priorities? If your evenings disappear in dishes and laundry, then you need to rethink your systems. Can you afford to hire help? How about asking family members to pitch in? Can you delay laundry until the weekend (or does that make weekends worse)? Throughout the book you'll find suggestions on making the drudgery less time consuming, and this, too, will provide you with additional time for your priorities.

For work priorities, try the following exercise: Write down a short definition of your job and your three top priorities. Then list the three primary items that occupied your day. Is there any overlap? If you're spending too much time on projects that don't fit in with your primary job priorities, work on redirecting your efforts as soon as possible. Work habits can be improved by using many of the techniques provided in this book. If you've been prevented from spending meaningful time on your "real" work by other people dictating your priorities, you may need to meet with your boss so that the two of you can reassess your priorities. Improving your work situation should make you more productive and a better employee, which may, in turn, fit in with long-term goals of moving ahead in your job.

Update your life. You may have agreed to serve on a community board several years ago when you had the time and the interest. Or you may have played tennis with your "college gang," and yet you're now far better than they are. Have you lost your enthusiasm? Is it taking up too much of your time? Drop or delegate the activities that are the *least* satisfying to you.

If you're like most of my clients, you've slipped into a lifestyle where you've given up some control. Instead of resigning from a volunteer committee you no longer enjoy, you continue with it because continuing seems easier than quitting (until the next time they need a big chunk of your time). Or you may continue to try to live up to family expectations that no longer fit with your schedule now that you have children (making a twelve-hour drive over Thanksgiving weekend has become exceedingly stressful, for example), but you think it's easier than asking everyone to create a new family tradition. Once it's no longer fun, quit if you can or modify it so that it keeps on being something you enjoy.

By reevaluating your life, you'll realize what is still important and what you can trim or adjust to make time for the new things that interest you.

WHEN YOU'RE FEELING REALLY OVERWHELMED

The world is demanding more of you than you can possibly do, and you feel as though your head is spinning. What to do?

Excuse yourself from your present environment (take a walk, fix a cup of tea, etc.) and take time to think. If you give yourself some distance and some time for making decisions, you'll have the clarity of thought that will permit you to do what's right:

- Does your daughter really need to be driven to a mall thirty minutes away on the weekend before Christmas?

- You have a report due, so how about meeting friends at the end of the week instead of when you're overwhelmed, trying to get your work done?

- You'd promised to drive to the next town to visit your aunt for the weekend, but since it snowed twelve inches on Thursday with more predicted over the weekend, wouldn't it make sense to tell her you'll make it the following weekend?

So often when we're feeling overwhelmed, we forget to give ourselves a break. "Staying on schedule" or "not disappointing" takes precedence over good sense. The result is added stress on you. Life in the nineties is stressful enough; keep reading for more advice on saying no.

Step 5. Simplifying Your Life

Life today is too complex. Even a simple decision, like getting in touch with someone, brings with it a host of decisions: Should you fax, phone, or e-mail the person? Or should you simply write them a letter?

Anytime you can make things simpler, do it. Here's some advice to get you started.

Whenever you're feeling bogged down by something ask:

- **Is this really necessary?** Just because you've always sent holiday greetings to people you used to know doesn't mean you still should. Look through your list. How many do you still hear from? How many would you want to hear from? Who on this list are you likely to want to see ever again? Or maybe you dread sending out any cards. If so, eliminate them this year. You can make a new decision about sending them next year.

- **"Isn't there a simpler way to do this?"** For example, you probably can have a present for a friend wrapped by the store where you're buying it; better yet, if you know what you want, phone ahead and have them wrap it and send it to you. Or if you're purchasing an item that notes "some assembly required," ask the store if it could be assembled for you. Quality stores will often do it for free; others may do it for a charge. Here are some other examples:

TASK	SIMPLE	SIMPLER
Provide cupcakes for bake sale	Make from mix	Buy from bakery or at grocery
Clean garage	Get your kids to help	Hire a teen
Have a casual party	Ask everyone to bring a dish	Order in Chinese
Purchase trash bags	Buy in bulk	Shop by mail order (and still buy in bulk!)
Launder your clothes	Take to laundry	Find a laundry service that picks up and delivers

- These are just a few of the types of tasks that can be made easier, less time-consuming, and therefore, less stressful. Refer also to Chapter 23 for a vast number of suggestions on how to do many of life's less interesting tasks faster and make them easier.

Tasks that should be simplified are the ones that are mundane, boring, and tiresome as well as those tasks that sound fun in the beginning but grow old fast. However, we all have tasks we enjoy despite the time and effort they take. You may love baking bread from scratch, hand-polishing your car, weeding your garden, or tinkering around to fix the latch on the back gate. Each person has tasks that can be difficult and time-consuming, but from which he or she derives enormous pleasure. If it's complex but important to you, then by all means keep doing it!

Step 6. Learning to Say No

Every magazine article and book on time management discusses the fact that you have to learn to say no, but few discuss how to set the boundaries for what it is you're going to say no to. In order to recognize something that truly deserves a no, you've got to go back to your priorities. If it doesn't fall within your new plans for yourself and if it isn't something you're absolutely obligated to do (and doesn't even sound fun), then don't do it. You can't manage your time if you give it away to everybody else.

One of my clients wanted to spend more time with his young children, so he made a rule for himself: "I will not attend evening meetings." How simple. By pinpointing the block of time that he wanted to devote to his children, he was able to come up with a system he could follow. It doesn't matter who calls or what they need, if they can't meet with him during the day, he simply says, "I'm sorry, but no." Other people find that they want to preserve Sundays for themselves and their family.

They may attend a religious service, but otherwise no is the answer to any and all requests for the day. In addition, try the following:

- Avoid looking like a good prospect for work that needs to be done. If your plate is full, don't get involved in conversations where you sense that a new committee is going to be formed to "look into the matter."

- When confronted with a request, consider the cost of saying yes. How many hours will that single word cost you? The more resolute you are, the easier you'll find it to express your inability to help out.

- Saying no to people to whom you've been saying yes for a long time is never easy. In doing a comparison check between your goals and your time demands, you can probably come up with a list of activities you'd like to phase out of your life. Write them down:

PHASE-OUT LIST

1.

2.

3.

4.

If you have mentally prepared yourself for the fact that no should be the response the next time they call, then uttering the word should be easier to do.

Friendly No's and How to Say Them

Helping out and helping others makes us feel good about who we are, and that's why it's so difficult when someone requests something of us. Without thinking, we say: "Yes, I'll stuff envelopes for a favorite charitable organization tomorrow." "Yes, I'll run an errand for a neighbor who has been ill." "Yes, I'll leave the car for an oil change." "Yes, I'll pick up the kids after the game." Before you know it, your day is filled with the priorities of others.

Try one or all of these five strategies for offering a friendly but firm no:

1. State your case. If you're really overburdened, no one who cares about you will want to push you over the edge. For example, rather than react in the heat of the moment to a child's request to be taken swimming ("How can you ask me to do that now? Can't you see how much I have to do for this party?"), pause for a moment and explain that you're really busy because twenty-five people are arriving at your home in two hours; you just won't be able to do it today.

With a spouse or an employer, you may be better off setting aside a few minutes to discuss all that must be done in the coming week or month and come up with a mutually agreeable plan for getting it done.

2. Offer options. If a person really needs something *now*, devote a few minutes to helping them plan a new strategy. If you can't help them, who can? Your spouse might not have thought of hiring someone else to fix the garage door, and that removes an item from your to-do list. Volunteer organizations are often as delighted to learn of a new person whom they might recruit as they would be if you—an old standby—helped out.

3. Offer future help. Many times our no doesn't mean "never," it just means "not now." Explain that and offer times when you might be willing to do what is requested.

4. Renegotiate. At both home and work, there are times when you simply must take another look at who does what. Renegotiations should be discussed at a time that is set aside for that purpose. In a marriage, your lifestyle may have changed in such a way (new town, different work hours, etc.) that family responsibilities should be redistributed. At work, you may need to schedule a meeting with your boss to discuss your dilemma. He or she may have no idea of the burden you are carrying. You may eventually find yourself with a new assistant to help your growing department, or you may find that there were other people on whom you can rely for some of the backup work that you need. In any case, if you open this type of discussion with the intent of finding a way to be an even more valuable employee, no boss will be sorry that you've brought it up.

5. Be firm. Even kids know when a no can be turned into a yes. Keep reminding yourself of why you didn't want to do it to begin with.

Here are some examples of how these strategies might help you:

ASKER	REQUEST	SUGGESTED RESPONSES
Your boss	Adds an urgent assignment and you're already drowning	Accept the new assignment, but draw up a list of your workload and ask for a meeting. Request that the two of you work together to establish new priorities. Your boss may reassign some of your tasks to someone else, or may at least free you of feeling that every-thing must be done *today*.

ASKER	REQUEST	SUGGESTED RESPONSES
Your boss	Asks that you work late tonight; you had family plans	Unless you already know that this is a must-do emergency, answer honestly that you're expected elsewhere, but offer to come in early to finish the project.
A co-worker	Requests help, and he's helped you out countless times.	If you're jammed up with your own work, offer an option: "I absolutely can't right now, but could I meet you at five p.m. or could we do it first thing tomorrow?"
Aging relative	Wants you to come by for a visit on Sunday, but you're committed to coaching a child's soccer game	"We won't be able to stop by, but why don't you come with us? Sarah would love it if you saw her play."
	Needs you to help select new washing machine	"I can't meet you to-day, but I'd be happy to do it Saturday."
	Needs driveway cleared of snow	"I need to get to work this morning, but I'm going to send over the teen who helped me with mine."

ASKER	REQUEST	SUGGESTED RESPONSES
	Wants you to partici-pate in gift selec-tions each year	Plan ahead and schedule it at your convenience: "I've got to pick up some-thing at the mall on Saturday. Come with me, and we'll do your shopping then."
Your child	Go to the toy store *today*.	"Not today, but write it on your wish list, and we'll go when I have time on Sat-urday."
	Needs a ride to the game; "everybody is going . . ."	Suggest strategies: "I can't drive tonight, but if Tom's father will, I'll do it next week." Or: "Could you go with Mary? The two of you could walk over."
Your spouse	Extra errands, doing repairs, or waiting at home for someone else to do them	Your marriage should be able to withstand a good number of "I'll have to do it tomorrow's," but if the tensions are increasing, schedule a time to renegotiate. Respon-sibilities need to be redistributed.

ASKER	REQUEST	SUGGESTED RESPONSES
Volunteer organization	Needs your time!	Offer options: "I can't do it this month, but I could help out next month." Or: "I can't do it, but my new neighbor is looking for ways to get involved."

Checkpoint and Review

Are you feeling less overwhelmed? Now that you've read this chapter, you have a personal framework for gaining more time. Remember:

1. Refer to your goal sheets regularly. They are your personal map to feeling calmer and less overwhelmed.

Update them as necessary. Perhaps one of your goals was joining a health club, but after researching them, you may decide you'd rather have a treadmill in your basement. Add a new short-term goal of saving the money to buy one.

2. Establish a priority system for what is most important to you, and then keep on track.

3. Keep a time sheet periodically. It will help you better understand where your time goes.

Keeping a time sheet needn't be a temporary exercise. For many clients I recommend that they do it over the course of a month; whenever they get bogged down; or right before a follow-up session with me. Periodic time checks will let you see how you're progressing at managing your time.

4. Always reduce and simplify. You should now have two new questions to guide you:

Whenever you're feeling bogged down, ask:

- Is this really necessary?
- Is there a simpler way of doing this?

5. Remember that it's okay to say no.

Saying no has to become one of your new priorities. If you don't stake out your claim to yourself, no one else will do it for you, so it's vital that you protect your time. Review the techniques of the friendly but firm no.

Don't expect miracles. Changes that last occur over a period of time. (Crash diets never work, and neither do crash time-management plans.) If six months down the line you see that you've dropped one of your outside activities that had begun to bore you, and that you've actually begun to say no a little more often, then you're making long-term changes that will benefit you for the rest of your life.

CHAPTER 7

· · · · · · · ·

More about Setting Priorities and Finding the Time

Mary was a business executive who understood many aspects of time management, and she employed a good number of them in her daily life. She had a good calendar system, never missed an appointment, and seemed to know how to keep interruptions to a minimum. When the company where she worked hired me, I was rather surprised to find that Mary was one of several people with whom I was to consult.

After learning more about her work habits, I saw that Mary failed to implement one of the fundamental elements of time management—she never set priorities. Despite rising early to take the train into the city and have time to herself in the morning, she didn't have a plan for herself—her early morning hours were often spent clearing her desk and updating her calendar and to-do list. Once she felt organized, she would pull out a client folder to begin work, only to discover all her quiet time had disappeared in getting organized. Needless to say, Mary had become quite frustrated at her inability to get things done.

I discovered another case of missing priorities when I was hired by a woman who wanted help in organizing her home.

When we met, I discovered a major source of household friction. She and her husband had divided household responsibilities, but he never seemed to get around to his—which largely had to do with household maintenance and upkeep. Despite having made the commitment to do his part, he never made it a priority, claiming he never had the time.

Even people who are normally good at setting priorities can lose it when they become overwhelmed. (And those who stay in control at the office often find they have difficulty coping at home.) Anyone from a mother with young children to an executive in an office can get to the point that there are so many demands on their time that they don't know what to do first. A very clear symptom of being overwhelmed is being unable to distinguish what items are more important. It feels like everything is closing in on you, and that everything must be done at the same time.

This chapter will guide you in the following:

- Bringing priorities front and center

- Acknowledging your prime time

- Establishing personal appointments

- Finding more time

Why It's So Hard to Do the Priorities

We're all human, and if left to our own preferences, we would all choose to do:

- A task we enjoy over one we don't enjoy

- A task that brings an immediate reward (if I return this phone call, I can cross it off my list even if I don't reach the person) versus one with delayed gratification (I need to work really hard on this speech I'm giving in two weeks, so people will enjoy it and I'll feel happy that it went well)

- A task that is simple (it's easy to alphabetize file folders) versus one that is hard (it's difficult to go through old files in a storeroom, reading through them and making a judgment on what to toss and what to save)

- The familiar (I'm used to having our old friends over for Sunday night supper) over the new (I'd be nervous about having a whole new group here for dinner)

- A task with a guarantee (that committee always does a great job, I'd be glad to be on it) versus something with a questionable outcome (that's a new area and no one has ever done that before; I don't know if it will work out)

This chapter will help you break out of this mold and focus on what's most important.

Bringing Priorities Front and Center

Within your master notebook (or your computerized to-do list), there are many types of tasks—some much more important than others. Scan through the items you've listed.

At home, the most important tasks are generally dictated by upcoming events. If you're having company for dinner, then cooking is a top priority. If the washing machine is on the blink, then getting it repaired or shopping for a new one must be taken care of. If you're leaving on vacation tomorrow, then packing is your number one activity. You should also have in mind long-term priorities. Tasks such as shopping in advance for the holidays, getting the chimney cleaned when the weather warms up, or reorganizing the kitchen cabinets for better space management (so that you can find things more quickly) are important. By accomplishing them in an orderly manner—so that nothing becomes a crisis—it will permit you to better manage your time.

At work, your top priorities should be those that lead to

more productivity, higher sales, or a better-run department—something that contributes to the success of the company. Keeping up with day-to-day tasks like taking phone calls or processing the mail must be done at some point, but should be worked into the overall priorities for the day.

As you go through your master notebook, put a red asterisk next to those items that take priority. This will remind you to put them on your daily to-do list as soon as possible.

As for your daily list, each item you select to be done on a given day should be ranked in order of priority. In general, you should expect to work on no more than two top-priority items per day (you'll either run out of time or run out of energy before you can tackle more). The other items on your to-do list should be more basic projects that do not require a big block of time and/or a high level of concentration.

Once you've identified what your top priorities are, you'll be able to schedule them for peak productivity periods. You'll soon find that you're feeling less overwhelmed because, at last, you're getting some of the things that are most important done.

"EVERYTHING IS A TOP PRIORITY!"

I hear this from clients all the time. But the reality is that not everything has the same importance. If you're unable to distinguish what your current priorities are, here's what to do:

1. Focus on just one day at a time for now.
2. Ask yourself: "What do I *really* need to work on today?"
3. If you still have too many tasks listed on today's priority list, look at the list and consider which tasks will have the most negative consequences if left undone: "If I don't get _____ done, the consequence will be _____." This should pare your list down to a more manageable number.
4. The items that have to be dropped from today's priority list should be rescheduled for a specific day. This helps

you avoid the last-minute panic of not having hand-outs for a program ready or delaying preparation for a business trip.

If you're still having difficulty establishing your priorities, talk it out with someone. At work, a fellow employee can be a good sounding board as you try to identify what's most important; at home, a spouse or a good friend can be very helpful. (When I am contacted by clients, I frequently serve this purpose. They need someone objective who can help them see their way out of an unproductive cycle.)

Setting Priorities (Again)

You've marked up your notebook with red asterisks and made note of what your priorities are. So now you know about priorities, right? Not quite.

When I work with clients, I show them that priority setting must be done constantly. Along with death and taxes, the one thing guaranteed in life is change. Our world is constantly shifting, and in order to make the best use of our time, we need to be prepared to manage what comes our way.

One day I was working with a client whose main priority of the day was creating a marketing plan for a new product. While I was there, her boss dropped in to tell her that the date for a big meeting in which she was to present some information had been moved up a week. What did she do? Switched priorities, of course. I helped her with three time-management steps that needed to be taken care of:

1. We mapped out a schedule and a plan for preparing for the meeting.
2. We made a point of collecting and filing in one place all the materials she needed for the marketing plan on which she had been working.
3. We selected a time on her calendar when she should be

able to return to the project that had originally been that day's top priority.

Too often people miss the second and third steps. An emergency comes up and they respond to it, leaving their current project without even putting away the materials. As a result, any thoughts they had and any work they had done on the project are lost.

Other people become angry about a scheduling change and storm around explaining how they had it all planned out so that they could finish their work, and now something has happened to prevent that. While there's no doubt that it's irritating to have to switch plans, responding in anger is self-defeating. There's not much you can do about a boss with an urgent request, or a child with a high fever, or even a pleasant priority switch like dropping everything because an old roommate from out of town dropped by. Being irritated or angry about not finishing the task you had set for yourself takes energy and accomplishes nothing, so the next time this happens, work *with* time instead of against it. Think to yourself: "I was supposed to do _____ today, but now something has come up. I'll reschedule it for another day so that I can focus fully on what has become my new priority."

At home, shifting priorities can be equally difficult, largely because these priorities often involve a high level of emotion. You may have promised to take your nine-year-old skating, but when her two-year-old brother develops an ear infection and needs to see a doctor, what's a mother or father to do? You're on your way to the doctor's, of course.

But, like a priority shift in the workplace, certain steps are necessary:

1. Shift to the most pressing priority.
2. Reschedule a time for what was to have been your priority.

Sometimes a schedule change may mean missing a child's soccer game or being unable to use the circus tickets you've purchased. Difficult as it is, talk to your child about why priorities had to be shifted, and together come up with a substitute activity that is satisfactory to all. Playing soccer with your child Sunday afternoon might compensate for missing Saturday's game. Missing the circus might be made up for by going to the child's favorite restaurant or selecting another special event to attend.

HOW TO BE PRIORITY SMART

1. Don't let the frivolous demands of others keep you from achieving your goals.
2. Always keep your own priorities foremost in your mind.
3. A priority is something you do first, not last.
4. If you focus on it, a priority will keep you centered and directed.
5. If your priority conflicts with that of a family member or your boss, it's time for a meeting of the minds.
6. Acknowledge that priorities can change due to time constraints and situations beyond your control.

Identify Your Personal Prime Time

By early adulthood most of us know whether we're larks (people who like to get up and who function particularly well in the morning) or owls (people who don't like to see the world before noon and who really come alive at night). Despite knowing this about themselves, most people don't know how to make the knowledge work for them when it comes to time management.

Every person has a metabolic high when they have more energy. Scheduling priority tasks during this peak time is the key to doing your best work most efficiently. Your thoughts will be clearer, and you'll be able to execute them more rapidly.

There are two steps to take to discover your prime time.

First, consult the daily time log you kept in Chapter 6. In all likelihood, your days will show a pattern, with more intensive work being accomplished either early or late. If you've felt that these days were basically in tune with the way you like to work, then you've established your first clue as to your "lark" or "owl" status.

Next, take the following quiz by circling the items that sound the most like you:

ARE YOU A LARK OR AN OWL?

LARK	OWL
Do you get up by eight even on the weekends?	Is morning wake-up difficult for you?
Do you enjoy getting a lot accomplished early in the day?	Are your best mornings ones that start slowly?
Do you try to fit in exercise early rather than late?	Are you an end-of-day exerciser?
Does the thought of staying out past ten-thirty give you pause?	Do you like afternoons or evenings better than mornings?
Do you fall asleep during the late news?	Is it easy for you to read for long stretches at night?

Based on your answers to the above, you should have a good idea of your peak performance period. Here are some guidelines on using it well.

Use your prime time for your most difficult task of the day. At the office, it may be writing up a report. At home, it may be organizing your financial documents for a tax preparer or coming up with a plan for a fund-raiser you promised to organize.

If you're a morning person, start on your task as one of the day's first undertakings. If you're a night owl who has to get up anyway, do low-level tasks until you're fully functioning, and then dive into the task at hand. (Owls should still try to get to their priorities as early as possible. As the day grows older, there is a decided increase in occurrences that will interfere with priority time.)

Set a specific start time, or the day will get away from you.

Don't waste your prime time. One client, a real early bird, used her precious morning hours at the office to return routine phone calls and finish with mail from the day before. After our consultation she realized how important it was to do those things in the afternoon, using her mornings for major tasks that required concentration.

If you do have to keep working past your peak productivity time, take a break and do something invigorating like walking around the block or phoning a friend who always makes you laugh. You'll return to the task feeling refreshed and energetic enough to see it through to completion.

Make Appointments with Yourself

Here's a common lament I hear from clients: "The phone rings; someone drops in with a question; some minor occurrence creates an emergency I have to handle. I never have time to work on what's *really* important!"

The solution? Take care of yourself first.

At the beginning of the week when you plan out your schedule and select what projects you'd like to undertake, make an appointment with yourself. Here are some suggestions:

- A regular appointment is preferable. If you know that every morning from 8–8:45 A.M. is to be devoted to something that is important to you, then it's the simplest type of appointment to safeguard. You'll never "forget" and schedule something at that time, because it's easy to remember that time slot is yours.

- To achieve this special time, consider going to the office when things are still quiet. Some business people do the reverse: They stay at home until ten doing work that requires concentration or returning important phone calls. "Then when I get to the office I'm available for all the crises that are destined to occur that day," says a retail executive whose children are grown. "I've done some of the work that is most important to me, so I'm ready to cope with what's new."

- Some people remove themselves from their normal environment for this appointment. They go to the library or find a conference room at the office where they can work uninterrupted for the allotted time.

- If a regular appointment is unthinkable because of your schedule, then scan your week. How many days can you schedule even as few as twenty minutes for yourself? Block those times in by writing it down in your calendar as if it were a medical appointment.

- A benefit offered by computer planners is that once the appointment is there, your week-at-a-glance calendar view will show that this time is unavailable for other appointments. That way you won't even *think* of breaking your appointment with yourself!

- Get into the habit of finding time for yourself every week. You'll soon feel more in control because the work that is important to you will be getting done, and that will be very satisfying.

- See Chapter 17 for suggestions on keeping interruptions to a minimum.

Creating More Time

Most of my clients find that they still need more time. You can add hours to your day by getting up early. When you read interviews with novelists, a large number of them write in the early morning before leaving home to go to their regular job. That's good time management! They found time for doing something that was very important to them.

Other people use those early morning hours to prepare for a running start once the rest of the household is up. They exercise, take care of household tasks, read the newspaper, and anything else that makes them feel relaxed and prepared for the day. That time is "their morning cup of coffee"—they'd be lost without it.

How much earlier should you arise? You'll be surprised what an extra fifteen to thirty minutes can do for your day! To figure the extra time you'd like to have, take into account the following:

Current waking time _____

Current bedtime _____

General number of hours of sleep required _____

You may find that a shift in bedtime is necessary. Currently you may stay up to see the monologue on one of the late-night talk shows. What if you gave that up (you can tape it to view the next day if you want to) and started going to bed before the eleven o'clock news? This could give you more than an extra forty-five minutes of sleep time at night, providing you with forty-five "spendable" minutes in the morning. Now fill in the following.

My new goals are as follows:

Bedtime _____

Wake-up _____

Additional motivation for getting up early can be provided by planning to do something specific at that time. Whether it's going for a jog or writing that novel, if it's something specific—that you'd hate to miss—you'll find that it's easier to remain committed to your goal.

I've had clients who have gradually moved from a 7:30 A.M. wake-up to 5:00 A.M. However, if you do make such a drastic change, keep yourself highly motivated by remembering that this extra time permits you to have time for yourself.

One final tip: Do the best you can to maintain a schedule relatively close to these hours on the weekend. Scientific studies of body rhythms have shown that people function better when they sleep and wake at regular times seven days per week. What's more, a weekend morning is a wonderful time to use for something just for you.

Checkpoint and Review

1. Keep your priorities front and center.

- Mark top priorities in your master notebook with a red asterisk.

- When you create your daily to-do list, select no more than two top priorities and schedule them for peak productivity periods.

- If everything is a top priority, review your list, making the best decisions you can about what needs to be done. If you're still having difficulty, use a co-worker or a friend to talk it through.

- Be prepared to shift priorities as needed, and reschedule what must be delayed.

2. Identify whether you are a lark or an owl in order to find your peak performance periods.

- Use your peak periods for top-priority work, and don't waste this prime time!

3. Make appointments with yourself to be certain that this prime time is available to you.

- A regular daily appointment is best, but erratic blocks of twenty to thirty minutes are better than nothing at all.

4. Create more time by getting up earlier.

- Shift your waking time gradually and gain anywhere from an extra fifteen minutes to an hour per day.

CHAPTER 8

• • • • • • • •

Getting It Done!

When it comes to getting it done, people approach a task in all sorts of ways:

John is a new young employee with a lot of promise, but he brings with him baggage that he has carried around since grade school: When his boss gives him a long-term assignment, he gets started immediately only to drift away and not return to it until the night before it's due—*crisis time*.

Crisis Time: They don't mean to create crises, but once it happens, they claim: "I work best under pressure." They're wrong. No one works best when they are stressed out and don't have time to re-work or review what they are doing. When it comes to task management, crises are to be avoided whenever possible!

Sue always feels overwhelmed, and yet when someone asks her to do something, she often says yes. The problem is she can't possibly juggle everything. But Sue just *can't say "no."*

Can't Say No: This style is often exhibited by what I call "The Superwoman" who tries to do it all. She's totally unaware of limitations—her own or others—and if she stays on this path, she'll end up overworked, overtired, and overstressed.

Mark has a concentration problem: "Sometimes I'll be working on one project, and I'm haunted by the other things I need to get done that day. When I get overwhelmed like that I just can't focus." Mark suffers from the *"ping-pong effect."*

Cathy works from a great list system, and while she's efficient at accomplishing her top priorities, she feels guilty over the large number of other things she'd like to accomplish but never has time to do. Cathy needs to *be more realistic* about her expectations and kinder to herself in the process.

The Ping-Pong Effect: Without a plan and without a system, it's impossible to get things done. Your mind jumps from task to task, and your eye wanders from pile to pile. These people need to create a better work style, and while working, they need to keep focused on the task at hand.

Let's Be Realistic: Most people never get around to accomplishing even their top priorities. If Cathy has learned enough time-management skills to accomplish these, she should give herself a break on the little things (can she delegate or forget about them?). People like Cathy should feel extremely proud of what they are accomplishing!

Although each of these people takes a different approach to managing a task, the first three all suffer from a similar time-management problem: They aren't accomplishing what they should be—or hope to be—during the day. Even Cathy, who is quite efficient at her top one or two tasks, needs to learn more about time management because she's expecting too much of herself—she needs to be more realistic.

This chapter will show you how to approach a task so that it will get done. We'll look at

- Breaking a project down into steps

- Getting it done: A time-management method that works

- Quick tips for getting it done

Forget-This-Not:
Break Big Projects Down into Small Steps

The first step in any type of task management is dividing a project into manageable parts. It makes it more comprehensible, and it provides you with a blueprint of exactly what must be done.

If you've ever asked a child to clean up their room, you quickly learn this is an ineffective request. Yet if you say to a toddler, "Please put your blocks away," or to a teen: "Hang up all the clothes on your floor, please, and empty your wastebasket," you've provided them with specific, manageable tasks. The tools are clear (the toddler will need a container for the blocks; the teen will need hangers for the clothes and a garbage bag for the trash), and the exact expectations have been presented.

As adults we must perform this request clarification for ourselves. What does it really mean to be asked to be a trustee for an estate, or to be chairperson of a committee? And while something like preparing a speech, writing a report, or decorating for the holidays sounds relatively clear, it's only because these tasks are a little more familiar to us. Each one still needs to be broken down into something that can be accomplished in twenty-to-sixty-minute blocks of time, because realistically most of our lives must be lived in these smaller segments. (When was the last time you had a totally free afternoon?)

Once you begin to view any major undertaking as a series of small steps, it seems much less overwhelming. One of my favorite examples of making the complex look simple is demonstrated by the chefs who appear on television. Well prepared with all the ingredients diced and measured, they make fixing a complicated dish look extraordinarily easy because they've taken many little steps in advance of their television cooking time.

With practice, breaking down smaller tasks like "clean out file cabinet," "sort through videotapes," or "weed garden" will become second nature to you, and this experience will polish your skill for approaching the larger, more overwhelming tasks that we all face. Keep in mind that any task, no matter how large, remains perfectly achievable if you take it one step at a time.

Finding Step One

So how do you identify step one? For most, the first step relies on personal priorities, and it becomes the point from which every other step will follow in a timely and orderly way.

Sometimes people with the same goal will choose to take entirely different first steps. Here's an example. The Wilsons and the Smiths both live in an urban environment, and now that they have children, they're investigating a move to the suburbs.

Because each family has different priorities, they take different first steps. The Wilsons have friends in a nearby community and place a high priority on being near them. For that reason their next step is to contact a real estate agent who shows properties in that community.

The other family, the Smiths, are very concerned about which school system their children will attend, so their first step is to contact several real estate offices in several different communities. They ask that housing information and statistics on the schools be mailed to them before they actually start looking at homes. The Smiths will narrow their search by selecting one or two school systems that seem to fit their needs.

As this example shows, taking a first step marks your path for the details to follow. You simply take into account your priorities and value system, and your step-by-step plan will become clear to you.

Occasionally, various steps in any project must be done sequentially, so when you break a project down into steps, make note of any that must be accomplished in a particular order.

If You're Afraid of the First Step, Start in the Middle

With clients I find that sometimes it's very clear what the first step of a project is—they just don't want to do it. That's when it pays to start in the middle, choosing a part of the process with which you feel comfortable.

Many executives have difficulty writing things—from speeches to reports. When clients describe to me what the task is, I often observe that they are quite passionate about some aspect of what they have to say. "Start there," I counsel. Even if the interesting part is in the middle or at the end, begin where you feel you have the most to say. Once you get started, you'll soon find that the rest will take care of itself.

In other cases, skipping over the first step is actually prudent. One family was wrestling with the issue of an elderly aunt who had become too frail to continue living on her own. She had fallen twice, and there had been several other incidents that suggested living alone in the house where she had lived for thirty years was impractical and dangerous. Normally, talking to a person about a major life decision would be a likely first step, but this was a case where starting in the middle was the advisable route. The family began by investigating area nursing homes and adult living facilities, selecting the ones they felt were satisfactory. Next, they priced out what it would cost to have an aide come daily to her home. By the time they finally sat down with Aunt Helen for a difficult conversation, they had narrowed the choices and could present her with the opportunity to make her own decision based on optimum lifestyle and expense.

Other Ways of Getting Started

1. Set a time; just get started.
2. Start small, with any step that appeals to you.
3. Work on only a part of the task and in small units of time.
4. Build consistency. Fifteen to twenty minutes every day will build a rhythm that will keep you going.
5. Use a kitchen timer. Tell yourself, "I can do anything for twenty minutes." Set the timer and get started. When the bell goes off, stop. Chances are, you'll have gotten enough done that you'll have a good idea of what you want to do with your twenty minutes tomorrow.

6. Inspire yourself. Develop a positive attitude and keep focused on the benefits of getting the task accomplished.

7. Shock yourself. Ask, "What are the consequences if I don't get started?" The answer may jolt you into action.

8. Use a buddy system. Ask a friend or colleague to nudge you into action and check on your progress.

9. Ask for help. Work with someone else or create a team. You'll find the work will go more quickly and be more fun.

10. Promise yourself a reward for getting started.

BREAKING BAD HABITS

When it comes to time management, what's your worst habit? (Most of us have one!) Look at the daily time chart I recommended you keep in Chapter 6. If your chart is sufficiently detailed, you may be able to identify what you do as a prelude to a major task. Some charts show a string of phone calls that were made right before "getting down to business." Others may show that you were struck by a sudden need to file or clean the refrigerator right before working on that major task. What do *you* do?

Acknowledging a bad habit is an important step toward breaking it. We've discussed placing a priority on accomplishing anything difficult early in the day, and you may find more helpful information on breaking your habit by referring to the "Time Traps" section of the book.

Getting It Done:
A Time-Management Method That Works

I have a friend named Jean who is extremely productive. She always has a full plate of projects underway, yet if someone asks her to do something and she says yes, the project is undertaken and completed just as she said it would be. How does she do it? Early on, Jean learned a time-management technique that is very important—she learned how to create a method for organizing projects so that she could finish what she undertakes.

Jean also knows something else that each person needs to learn: she *knows herself*. She will say no when she is at the point that satisfaction at a job well done is turning into saturation from having too much to do. She knows her physical, mental, and time limitations and is willing to acknowledge them. To be efficient, here are some guidelines:

1. Set goals for what you can reasonably hope to accomplish. By establishing and reaching achievable goals, you'll be inspired to keep working because you'll see that it can be done. If you're cleaning out the basement, you're not likely to complete the task in a single afternoon, but it is reasonable to expect to finish reorganizing one set of shelves. Novelists often promise themselves that they'll write five pages per day, and though it may take months to finish an entire book, each day they can enjoy a feeling of accomplishment for having met their pages-per-day quota.

2. Take time to plan what you're going to do. By focusing on exactly what needs to be done, you'll identify the steps you need to take to see it through to completion. Note if any of the steps must be done in a particular order.

3. Create deadlines and interim checkpoints. You'll finish the entire basement by Thanksgiving; the special report for work will be completed in two weeks. Whatever the project, note down interim deadlines by each step so that you'll know if you're running ahead or falling behind.

4. Block out the time. Little tasks can be slotted into odd moments of a day; major tasks require setting aside blocks of time. Whether it's rewriting your résumé or cleaning out a closet, you need to set aside time to work on the project. Even twenty to thirty minutes of uninterrupted time can make all the difference. You'll also find that by establishing a set period of time in which to do a project, you'll be more efficient. If you give yourself a full afternoon to finish a one-hour task, you'll find that Parkinson's law will take over and the job will expand unnecessarily to fill the time.

5. Select a space for the undertaking. If it's a work-related project that should be done at your desk, you can make it easier by creating a clear space for you to work. If your home project is gift-wrapping for the holidays, you may want to set up a table in your family room or basement to get the job done.

6. Arrange to have the tools and materials you'll need close at hand. Before you begin, make certain you have what you'll need for the project. Too often people start a task and then find that they have to keep hopping up and down to get the things they need. If you're working on your taxes, you'll want your financial records, a calculator and/or the computer program with your financial data on it, and all the appropriate tax forms. If you're answering letters for work, be sure to have letterhead, envelopes, stamps (for a home office), and any additional papers you need. If you're hanging pictures at home, make certain you have the right nails and wire so you won't have to make a trip to the store.

7. Give the task your full attention. Full concentration is the golden key to getting things done. Whether it's cooking a meal or writing a lengthy business letter, the project will be completed more quickly if you focus fully.

8. Save a few minutes for cleaning up. Many of my clients think that if they are in the middle of preparing a report, the right thing to do is leave everything out on their desk until the next morning, when they'll work on it again. It's not a bad theory, but it never works in actual practice. Here's why: You're about to leave the office and the phone rings. You have to pull out a new file, and since there is no clear space to put it, you spread it across the materials on which you were just working. Then the phone rings again, and the caller provides you with some figures you need for something else. Now you have two open files and some additional notes on your desk. It's very likely that some papers will intermingle, and even if you guard against that, your original project has now been shoved around to the point that you're going to have to reorganize the papers in the morning. Make it a rule: *When your work time on a particular project ends, pick it up neatly and put it away.* Though leaving a project out for the next day sometimes seems like a good idea at the time, a clean work area is far more inspiring than one where you have to reassess where you were when you left off.

SELECTING THE RIGHT TIME
FOR GETTING OTHER TASKS DONE

In the last chapter we talked about using peak periods for top priorities. You're probably saying, "But what about everything else in life? When does that stuff get done?"

You do it at the right time for the task. Here are some guidelines:

- Establish a routine for any recurring task such as paying bills. Though you'll soon find that the activity on those dates becomes second nature, always put it on your planner. If your day has been filled with the unexpected, you have the written reminder of something you have to reschedule or get done.

- "Do it now" whenever you can. RSVP to invitations as they arrive. If you take "it" off, out, or put it down, then put it away. File meeting-related papers as soon as the meeting is over. Unpack parcels and groceries as soon as you get home. Do whatever you can to minimize a backlog of things to do.

- Don't leave household tasks undone. Make your bed first thing in the morning. Do the dishes right after a meal.

Take a damp paper towel (keep a roll under the bathroom sink) and wipe up after you've washed in the morning. Avoid putting off until tomorrow everything from a list of phone calls to a stack of laundry, a pack of reading material to yesterday's mail. If you take care of things as you go along, you won't have to make time to go back and pick up.

What's Undone All Too Often Remains Undone

My work brings me in contact with clients' true work habits. I get to see the boxes and bags that get hidden before the visitors arrive, and I hear office tales of why they just can't get anything done.

What I can tell you about my observations is that almost everyone hates finishing the same things. See if these projects left undone are the same projects that are stuffed in closets around your house or that haunt your desktop at the office.

Top Five Undone Household Projects

Other than "papers, papers, papers" (which are discussed in Section 4), here are five household projects that are frequently left undone:

1. Messy closets	"I meant to reorganize them!" is a lament I hear frequently. Start one closet at a time, and break it into steps. Attack the upper shelves first, moving next to the hanging area, and finally addressing the problems on the floor. You'll find things you'd forgotten about, and one more spacious closet will provide inspiration to go on.
2. Going through old magazines	The stacks grow higher and higher. When are you really going to have time to sort

through them? Your best bet is tossing all but the most recent issue of each magazine. Your second choice is to set aside a Saturday afternoon to sort through them, pulling any articles you really think you'll read. These can go in an "On the Go" reading file, while the rest of each magazine gets recycled or donated to hospitals, libraries, or schools.

3. Unsorted photographs

Few people succeed in putting together the family albums they dream of. To reform, start in the middle. The next photos you have developed should be labeled on the outside (that step is simple!), and use that batch for your first album entries. Later on, make it a priority to do the following:
1. Locate all your photographs and organize them by date.
2. Start putting them into albums.
If you make a commitment, you *can* get it done!

4. Unfiled recipes

The problem with clipping recipes is you need to establish a system for trying them. Here's what to do:
1. Purchase one of the specially designed recipe notebooks or a loose-leaf notebook and pocket dividers.
2. Use the pockets for the recipes you haven't tried, and don't mount the recipe on a page until after you've tried, and decided to keep, it. (Photocopy before mounting; it lasts longer.)
3. Clean out regularly. If you've clipped five beef stew recipes and still haven't tried one, sort through them, selecting only one or two to keep and try. Then set a date or an occasion when you will test it out.

5. Glueing/
   Fixing Projects

Basements are filled with good intentions. "If I just fix that leg, it will be a great chair." Or: "I could turn that light fixture into a flower bowl if I had a little time." Go through your good-intentions area and ask yourself some hard questions. If you do fix the chair, will it be sturdy enough for anyone of any weight to sit in? If you do turn the light fixture into a flower bowl, will anyone really want it? If you evaluate each item carefully, you will likely be able to narrow your collection considerably.

Top Five Undone Office Projects

People in offices have their weak spots, too.

1. Filing

No one likes to file! The best way to manage the task is by doing it a little bit at a time. I like to take five minutes at the end of the day to do my filing rather than devote twenty-five minutes once a week. Select a routine that works for you, and do it.

2. Mail

It arrives every single day, and it needs to be dealt with that often. Make a point of getting through all your mail daily so that you don't create a backlog. (See Chapter 14 for more suggestions.)

3. A major project

Throughout the chapter we've discussed how much easier it is to do a simple task first. If you take the chapter's suggestions to heart, you'll soon find that it's not so hard to dive into a major project early in the day, and put one or two steps of it behind you.

4. Reading

It's tough to find time to keep up with business reading. That's why you need to establish a time and a place when you do it. If you commute by public transportation, you have a built-in opportunity. If not, use moments like when you're waiting at the doctor's or for a child to finish a piano lesson, or select a lunchtime or an evening when you complete what you need to.

5. Organizing for others

Mary can't complete her report until she gets statistics from you. The sales department wants some special material for a new brochure. The boss needs some data for a speech. The list often seems endless. Requests from others need to be prioritized in order of importance, and then time should be set aside to meet the requests.

Ten Quick Tips on Getting It Done

- Keep a clean desk/work area. Starting out with a fresh slate each day means that you don't have yesterday's "history" to comb through, and your outlook will be brighter knowing that you're making a fresh start.

- Be selective about what you say yes to.

- Write down things you need to do. If you talk to successful people, they always mention that they are habitual about keeping a running list of tasks.

- Don't clog your brain trying to remember conversations and project details. If you're having ongoing discussions with someone about a certain issue, write down pertinent notes in your master notebook or your computerized "contact manager." When the discussion resumes again, you'll have a complete account of what has been agreed so far.

- If your office has a voice-mail system, this can be a great get-it-done method for leaving messages to yourself. No matter what time, simply pick up the phone and record your message. The reminder will be waiting for you when you're ready to retrieve it.

- Make it easy on yourself by establishing a pleasant environment for a disliked task. If you hate paying bills, plan to do it while listening to your favorite CD.

- When researching something, don't wait for that one last statistic or bit of information—you may wait forever. Determine a time when you'll move ahead with what you have. As you work, you'll either determine that the additional data isn't necessary, or you'll increase the pressure on the person who needs to help you get it.

- Be decisive. Most day-to-day decisions should be made quickly and easily. At the office, make quick decisions on everything that you can. Every job has enough of the "ponderables" that you'll have plenty of other things to think about. The same is true at home. Yes or no to attending the Smiths' Groundhog's Day party? Yes or no to the letter from the local wildlife preserve asking for money? The longer you wait to make up your mind on something, the more time and energy that are eaten up.

- Delegate what you can. See Chapter 9.

- If the task is really a burdensome one, plan on a reward for completing it. Small rewards like a new CD or a special movie rental from your video store for interim deadlines; large rewards like an evening out or a day at the beach for accomplishing a major task.

HASTE MAKES WASTE

Can you think of a time when you had to hurry to complete something—that harried, unable-to-concentrate feeling of rushing and just wanting it done?

Once you devote the time to a project, it's important to concentrate fully on the task at hand and to work carefully and methodically. Transposed numbers or carelessly written sentences will create trouble—and cost time—later on, so work at a pace that you are relatively certain you won't make a mistake.

You've set aside the time for the project. You've scheduled in time for the other important projects you need to do that day. You don't need to rush.

Checkpoint and Review

1. Break projects down into small steps.

- Identify step one and items that need to be accomplished sequentially.

- If appropriate, start in the middle.

2. Remember the get-it-done method that works:

- Set goals.

- Plan your project and identify necessary steps.

- Create deadlines and checkpoints.

- Set aside specific time.

- Select work space.

- Get tools and material needed.

- Focus fully.

- Save time for clean-up.

3. Select the right time for the task.

- Important projects need protected time.

- Routine projects can be slotted in throughout the day.

CHAPTER 9

· · · · · · · ·

Extra Help, Extra Time: Your Guide to Delegation

At a business meeting I met a man who made me wonder how he kept up with everything he did. He was editor of the town newspaper and on the board of seven different organizations. I asked him: "How can you possibly give time to so many organizations *and* run a newspaper?" His answer: "I delegate."

"If only I had an extra pair of hands . . ." How often have you said that? Yet how many times we resist help when it's there? At the office, I hear: "I am the only one who can handle that." "No one else understands how to do it." "I don't delegate because it takes too much time to explain."

At home, it's often the same. Parents or spouses end up taking back jobs they've tried to delegate, because the other person doesn't do it "their" way.

Both at home and the office, people often end up feeling: "By the time I supervise her doing the job, I might as well have done it myself."

The trick to getting and making good use of that extra pair of hands involves three things:

1. Giving the right task to the right person

2. Providing careful training to show how the job is to be done and monitoring progress along the way

3. Realizing that the transfer of responsibility doesn't happen overnight

In this chapter you will learn about finding the help you need both at home and at work. We'll examine:

- Family help

- Employed help

If you live alone and have no staff, keep reading because there are also lots of ideas for finding:

- Outside help

Family Help

They have to help because they are family, right? Ah, but are they artful at getting out of it! Do you recognize any of the following situations:

- The spouse on being confronted with the stack of dishes he took out of the dishwasher but neglected to put away: "Oh, I didn't put away those dishes because I didn't know where they went."

- The grammar-school child on being asked why only some of the breakfast dishes were put into the dishwasher: "I didn't know the dishes in the sink went into the dishwasher, too. I thought they were there for something else."

- The teen who announces: "Why should I have to pick it up (or put it away) when I didn't put it there!"

And feigned ignorance covers many bases:

- "I didn't hear you say you were going out to shovel snow."

- "I don't know how to start the washing machine."

- "Those aren't mine. I left them on her floor because I don't know *where* she keeps them."

- "I know we helped with the dishes last night. I didn't know you needed help tonight, too."

- "Oh, I didn't know you meant for me to take out the garbage *today*."

When it comes to helping around the house, family members often display such a lack of knowledge and amazement about how the household functions, it really leaves you wondering how they get to school or work every day.

Let this be the beginning of a new family system.

Taking Personal Responsibility

Forget about distributing chores for now. In all likelihood, you're wasting some of your time because someone in your house is shirking their personal responsibilities. (Many of my clients are spending so much time sifting through papers on a spouse's desk looking for a bill, or trying to find and then vacuum the carpet in their teenager's bedroom, that they haven't gotten as far as chores yet.)

Do you encounter situations like these: Your six-year-old never puts back toys after he plays with them. Your teen thinks that a "water world" atmosphere of damp floor and soaking towels enhances her "shower" experience. Your spouse seems incapable of carrying snack dishes back to the kitchen. Your first task in gaining extra time is going to be shifting the burden of personal responsibility back to them.

- Make a list of all the things you do for other family members that they could be doing for themselves. If your spouse shares household tasks, it may be the kids whom you both are overhelping. If so, both of you should make a list.

- Start slowly. Select one or two habits that you'd like to have each person change (laundry in the basket instead of on the floor; bed made in the morning; personal dishes cleared from the table after meals, etc.) and talk to them privately.

- Don't expect miracles, and do expect to remind them frequently while they learn this new habit.

- Establish consequences based on age and ability. A small deduction from the allowance of children school age and up can be effective. Take away a privilege for a week if they consistently ignore their responsibilities.

- Try a reward system. It's a great motivator for little ones and worth trying with a balky teen. Ten stars or check marks for a job well done can earn your child a small, age-appropriate reward; or promise a dinner featuring their favorite homemade meal when they reach the desired goal.

- Praise helpful behavior often.

- With another adult, work through why the task doesn't get done. (Adult reform is by far the most difficult.) Explain to them the why of your request (why you personally don't have time to stop at the shoemaker for them; why socks should go into the hamper right side out). If they understand your reasoning and can empathize with your situation, it may help. Or if they continue to forget, ask for suggestions as to what might help them remember. Moving a laundry basket inside a closet should make laundry-in-the-basket more likely, or perhaps a spouse is just never going to get those bills paid on time, so you might as well swap responsibilities.

In an ideal household, no one would have to pick up someone else's laundry, empty someone else's pockets before throwing jeans in the wash, bring other people's dishes to the kitchen, or pick up shoes or toys in the hallway. Though we all know that a state of perfection is difficult to reach, there's always room for improvement. Choose the responsibilities you want other family members to reassume, and then with love and patience keep reminding them.

Chores: Selecting Responsibilities

Whether two or four or ten of you live in a household, schedule a family meeting to discuss a redistribution of chores. For the meeting you'll need a list of daily chores (setting and clearing the table, washing dishes, making bed, laundry, etc.) and those that must be performed weekly (grocery shopping, dusting, vacuuming).

The successful worker is a happy worker, so ask if there are any particular chores anyone would like to volunteer for. A very young child won't be capable of carrying out garbage, so you'll want to limit their chores to age-appropriate assignments. Pre-school children are capable of one-step tasks (put markers away; tear up lettuce leaves for salad; put napkins on place mats) with an adult or older sibling working alongside them. Children ages five to nine can take responsibility for bed making and table clearing as well as brief tasks with you nearby in case they have questions. Children ages ten and up are capable of more complex tasks such as neatening a room and dusting it or running to the store for you.

Most children and teens prefer chores in which a benefit is realized: If I make the salad, we can eat it. If I fold the clothes, my new jeans will be available to wear again. Chores like dusting and vacuuming are less rewarding to kids because they don't understand what the big deal about dirt is anyway.

Should chores rotate? Here's a chart to help you decide what will work best for your family:

THE BENEFITS AND DRAWBACKS OF
ROTATING FAMILY CHORES

BENEFITS	DRAWBACKS
Provides variety and helps keep tasks from becoming boring	As kids become older and have more extracurricular activities, they often aren't home when many chores are done. A permanent assignment based on their time availability may work best.
Allows family members to learn all aspects of house management	When jobs rotate, it can become confusing as to who is responsible for what and when. If permanent jobs are assigned, it's always very clear who is responsible for taking out the trash.
If adult family members are part of the rotation, it permits an "expert" to do the chore really well occasionally.	Rotating chores denies everyone pride of ownership over a task. With consistency, the chore becomes that person's "territory," and often they'll come to care about how it's done.

If your family decides to make permanent assignments, establish a list with squares for checking off that the chore has been done. (The charts can be abandoned once it is proven that the child does the chore regularly.) A chart for a chore that must be done bi-weekly might look like this:

	2/22	2/25	2/29	3/5	3/8
Trash	✔	✔			

A daily chore might be charted like this:

	Mon.	Tues.	Wed.	Thurs.	Fri.	Sat.	Sun.
B'fast dishes	*done*	*done*	*done*				

If your family wants to rotate chores, this type of chart will help you keep track of responsibilities:

	Mon.	Tues.	Wed.	Thurs.	Fri.	Sat.	Sun.
Mom	*laundry*	*iron*	*laundry*	*general pickup*	*laundry*	*vacuum*	*free*
Dad	*dishes*	*free*	*dishes*	*vacuum kitchen*	*dishes*	*laundry*	*yard work*
Steve	*free*	*dishes*	*help w/ laundry*	*dishes*	*trash*	*dust*	*mow lawn*
Sue	*trash*	*vacuum kitchen*	*trash*	*light dusting*	*free*	*dishes*	*dishes*

Set a deadline for all chores. Family members should come to understand that on normal evenings, the dinner dishes are to be done by eight. When a load of laundry comes out of the dryer, your teen should be told the clothes must be folded within the next forty-five minutes (or whatever amount of time you feel is reasonable). Set a kitchen timer for forty-five minutes so they will be aware of the time that has passed.

Review job assignments as schedules change. You might find it helpful to expect a "job review" at the beginning of the summer and early fall. You may need to make some adjustments or reassignments at this time.

WHEN ALL ELSE FAILS . . .

1. No help with dinner? Refuse to cook. Being hungry may inspire them to figure out how to make a sandwich, or encourage them to pitch in and help with the dinner you'd planned.
2. Laundry never in the hamper? Quit washing the offending family member's clothing. A daughter will see the light the minute her navy sweater isn't ready for Saturday. A son will finally focus on it when all his shirts are gone.
3. Their bedrooms are totally out of control? Offer to help them by coming through with a garbage bag; anything on the floor goes out.
4. Dinner is late, the kids are bickering, the house is a mess. . . . Hand the keys to your spouse and say, "It's your turn. I'm taking off for a week." Let your partner figure out what needs to get done, who goes where, what they need, how to get them to doctor appointments, return class notes, set up play dates, and supervise school projects. The whole family will quickly learn how much it takes to run a household.

Helping Household Help (Non-Family Members)

When it comes to working well with household help (if you're lucky enough to have it), the most important thing is being clear about your expectations and careful in your job training.

Consider:

- Communicate what is important to you. If it's vital that they arrive on time so that you can leave for work, let them know that.

- Spend a day with cleaning help and at least a week with full-time child care help to show them how you like things done. After training, be available in case they have questions. Particularly with children, it is impossible to anticipate many situations that occur, so be available to comment on how you would like them to handle issues such as eating problems or tantrums.

- Communicate, communicate, communicate. When something is bothering you, don't be afraid to discuss it. If you catch things early, chances are you can alter the situation before it becomes a major issue.

Help at Work

Distributing tasks at work is important not only for freeing your time but also for building a stronger team. Your department will be smarter for having taught others some of what you know. At work:

- Decide what to delegate. If nothing comes to mind immediately, take a few days to consider what could be accomplished by others.

- Although passing on only boring tasks is a tremendous temptation, remember that your team will be more successful if you can inspire someone else to assume more responsibility. For that reason, select some tasks that will be more challenging.

- Who should take on the job? Match task to the ability or skills of someone to whom you can delegate.

- Train carefully and patiently.

- Create a sheet for yourself so that you can keep track of the work:

DELEGATION SHEET

Date	Name	Assignment	Due Date

Notes

- Teach your staff how to stay organized with their projects by using a similar log. Have them record the steps in a larger task, with interim deadlines so that they'll know if they are working on schedule.

- Be available for questions.

- Let them know that they should come to you if they encounter a major obstacle. (You don't want to be surprised with this type of news on the day the project is due.)

- If they run into difficulty, be patient. Help them figure out a solution. Taking back the job you've delegated is a mistake for you and a disservice to the employee.

TEACHING A TASK

Time and again people tell of asking someone to do something, and then eventually they take the job back from the person. "They just couldn't do it right," they say. The error is in the training. It's only natural that you would like a task performed a certain way, but to achieve what you want, you need to be very careful and specific in your instruction. Here's how to do it successfully:

1. Set aside uninterrupted time when you can explain the job. Whether it's teaching an assistant to sort the office mail or showing your teen how to bag the kitchen garbage, assume that you must explain everything—even aspects of the job that seem obvious to you. (Remember the list of family excuses about chores? Well, office workers can come up with some good ones, too.)

2. Break the job down into parts and clearly demonstrate each part. At home, washing the lettuce is helpful, but the job is incomplete if you don't teach how to dry it. At the office, telling the person to answer the phone is all well and good, but you need to instruct them as to what greeting they should use when answering the phone, how to handle questions, take messages, and if they have to put someone on hold, how often to check back with the person.

3. Demonstrate the job *exactly* the way you would like it to be done. Telling them to "sort the mail" and showing them how to do it will bring about vastly different results.

4. Show the person where they can get additional information or help if they need it. Showing them the whereabouts of instruction booklets or appropriate file resources may save you time later on.

5. Put them in charge, but let them know you're available if there are problems.

6. Compliment them on a job well done, regularly and often.

Outside Help

In today's busy world, many services are there just for the asking. Others may cost extra, but may be worth it. Here are fifteen ways to find all types of extra help.

- Patronize businesses that deliver whenever possible. That saves on your errand time.

- Why go to the post office and stand in line to mail a package? Phone one of the air-carrier-package companies who will, for a small fee, come to you to pick up parcels.

- In today's world, you needn't even leave your home or office for grooming. Personal-care consultants will come to you. (There are also some who will come to groom your dogs so you don't even have to drop off Fido for a day of beauty.)

- Most department stores now offer free tailoring on both men's and women's purchases. Take advantage of it.

- When purchasing a gift, request that the store wrap it for you.

- Better yet, patronize your favorite boutique or gift service company. When you need any type of gift, they'll listen to what you want and make suggestions as well. Once you've made your selection, they'll wrap and deliver it—all done over the phone.

- Look for special services. There are small service businesses springing up to do all types of things. See which of these may be available in your community:

  - "Carpool" vans for conveying children from place to place.

  - Party planners will arrange an entire event for adults or kids; all you have to do is show up.

  - "Elves" to help with holiday decorating and wrapping.

  - "Math wizards" to take over bill paying and checkbook balancing.

  - "Chefs in the making" will shop and prepare dinner for you and even clean up.

  - Organizers to help you straighten out everything from closets to kitchens and photographs to papers. The list is endless.

- If your child needs extra educational support, check out your in-school programs. Your tax dollars are already paying for it.

- You might also consider thinking of the task you need done and then looking for someone to do it. Area high schools offer a willing pool of kids who will help at parties, clean out garages, or mow lawns, and retired people may be just right for driving your mother to the doctor once a month. Seek out the help you need.

WHEN YOU'RE TRULY OVERWHELMED

Ask for help. That's something that's very difficult for many people to do, and the more overwhelmed you become, the more likely you are to resist—you're feeling tense and tired, and all you can think about is struggling through the rest of the dishes or the report for work so that you can, at last, relax.

Instead of your "nose to the grindstone" approach, lift your head for a moment, and think: "Who could help me out of this jam?" Call in the troops—your spouse, your kids, a neighbor, a colleague, or a friend. It may be time to call in a favor. Remember, if you don't ask, you don't get.

Checkpoint and Review

1. Teach family members to assume responsibility for themselves (taking into account their age). Start slowly by showing them what tasks you would like to have them assume.

- Don't expect miracles, but do be persistent in insisting that they be in charge of themselves.

2. Distribute family chores based on interest, ability, and time availability.

- Teach the chores slowly and carefully.
- Establish a check-off system for completed tasks.

3. With household help, make your expectations very clear.

- Be available for training.
- Address mild irritations before they become major annoyances.

4. Build a stronger office team by delegating work.

- Match the task to the ability or skills of the person.
- Train carefully.
- Create a delegation sheet for yourself and have the person keep his or her own so that there is a way to keep track of the work.

5. To teach a task at home or at work:

- Set aside time to explain the task.
- Break the job down into parts.
- Demonstrate the task exactly as you want it done.
- Show the person where additional information for the task is kept.
- Supervise the task.
- Let them do the task alone, but let them know you're available if there are questions.
- Provide them with positive feedback.

6. Look for outside services to help you.

- Utilize free services offered by businesses you patronize.
- Hire others to do what is time-consuming or boring for you.

7. When you're truly overwhelmed, *ask for help*!

CHAPTER 10

· · · · · · ·

Getting There on Time

Overwhelmingly Bad Excuses for Being Late

Tardiness always calls for an explanation. You're probably in bad shape if you've used any of the following reasons for being late:

- "I'm sorry I'm late. We had a rabid raccoon in our backyard."

- "Sorry we're an hour late. We forgot to turn the clocks ahead."

- "The train was delayed because there was a dog on the tracks."

- "Just as I got the baby in her snowsuit, she needed a clean diaper, and then I discovered her outfit was wet. By the time I changed her, she was hungry, so I had to stop to feed her. When I fed her, she got some of the formula on my blouse, so then I had to change, and then I had to put her in her snowsuit again, and *that's* why we're late. I'm glad I don't have twins."

■ "To tell you the truth, I'm *always* late. I'm usually jumping into the shower just as the rest of the family announces that it's time to leave."

I can't think of "late" without being reminded of a couple who had planned a two-week vacation with their children. They were traveling by plane, and everyone was excited. Traveling with a family requires a lot of gear, and husband and wife split their to-pack lists and worked doggedly to get ready for this long-planned trip. They were quite proud of themselves as they settled back into the seats of the cab on the way to the airport—only to have their pleasure dashed upon arriving at the airport check-in counter and being told they were a *full day late* for their flight!

Anyone who has ever run late for a plane or a really important meeting, or anyone who runs late in the morning, knows the heart-pounding, palm-sweating feeling of panic as you try to will your car (or the train or bus) to go faster and faster. You feel pressured, knowing you don't have time for a red light, a dropped glove, or any kind of unexpected delay. The anxiety over still trying to be there more or less on time leaves you feeling frustrated, irritable, and angry.

I understand running late; I hear about it all the time. I have a client who arrived late for her own wedding, and then almost missed the plane for her honeymoon—neither she nor her new husband had packed, so they had to stop at home to pick up "a few things" before leaving for the airport!

My client's story illustrates what often goes wrong in trying to get to places on time. Most people practice "at the door" planning. Tasks that could be done in advance (whether packing for a honeymoon or organizing your briefcase for the day) are left to the last minute, making anyone feel overwhelmed by everything that must be done before walking out the door.

In this chapter you'll learn how to place a priority on promptness and how to get everywhere on time.

> *Remember, being late means there is*
> *someone somewhere waiting for you.*

Promptness as a Priority

If you have trouble getting places on time, chances are you're like most of my clients. They intend to be prompt, but they have not yet made it a priority. They take those extra few minutes to finish the newspaper in the morning, or they answer that one last call before leaving work for an appointment. Without thinking, they've given up control of their time. Finishing that one last article in the newspaper means you have no buffer time for bad traffic. The phone call that should have taken just a second leads to a promise from you that you'll fax the caller something right away, so after the phone call is over, you've got to find the piece of paper that must be faxed. One thing leads to another, and the next thing you know, you're late.

What I teach clients is that they needn't put themselves through the stress of being late. What's more, being on time makes a strong personal statement. It presents you as a person who is in control and should be taken seriously.

> *To avoid feeing overwhelmed (and late),*
> *you have to take charge of your time.*

One way to motivate yourself to make promptness a priority might involve focusing on what will happen if you *are* late. Here are some faces most people wouldn't want to see if they are running late:

THE FACE	THE SITUATION
The traffic cop	When you were speeding to make up some time.
Your mother	At her fiftieth-wedding anniversary party
Your five-year-old	When you're late picking her up at school
Your spouse	Whom you've arranged to meet on a street corner
Your sister	Who is taking you to the symphony for your birthday
Your friends	Who are waiting for you at a restaurant, and the host won't seat anyone until the entire party is there
Your therapist	Who insists that you must be avoiding therapy since you always arrive late!
Your boss	At your job review
The IRS agent	At your audit

If you've made the commitment to be somewhere, then it's important that you commit to being there on time. Now you must make promptness a priority.

Six Principles of Promptness

1. Plan ahead. Don't practice at-the-door planning, and don't leave tasks to the last minute. Whether it's laying out breakfast dishes and your clothing the night before or preparing in advance for a meeting, do as much as you can ahead of time. The more tasks you have to accomplish prior to any type of departure, the more likely you are to be late.

2. Create an orderly environment. Of course, you can't find your keys if they are under all those papers. And what about the library books, weren't they over there? At work, the agenda for the meeting must have arrived in yesterday's mail, or was it the day before . . . it must be here somewhere. . . .

Elsewhere in the book (see the "Time Traps" section), I point out that you can save time instantly by bringing order to your environment, and this is particularly true when it comes to getting places on time.

At home:

- Establish a set place for your possessions, and don't ever put them anywhere else. Although keys are the most vivid example of an item that needs a permanent "home," order throughout the household is important. Whether you're looking for a library book or your child's permission slip for the field trip at school, you need to establish places where you keep the things you'll need.

- Near the door by which you exit, establish a table or a chair where you can place items you'll need when you leave. Whether it's a package for the post office or an umbrella you think you'll need, having a spot where you can leave things for your departure helps to get organized.

At work:

- Establish files for out-of-your-office meetings. For example, if you attend a monthly planning meeting, have a permanent file for information relating to that committee. That way whenever you receive a pertinent piece of information, it can go directly into the file.

- Keep your briefcase by your desk. As the day progresses, put items you need with you into your briefcase as you think of them. When it's time to leave the office your briefcase is already packed and ready to go.

3. Establish helpful routines. Anyone who has moved recently knows the feeling of losing "routine"—as when your hand automatically reaches for a coat hook that isn't there. It's amazing what our bodies learn to do without thinking. The more routines you can build into your exits (and entrances, because that's when you place keys, put down gloves or your train pass, and hang up coats), the easier you'll find it to exit on time.

4. Determine at what time you need to begin getting ready. Whether you're leaving for work in the morning or for a dentist appointment at midday, getting places on time is largely a mathematical exercise. You must add travel time to preparation time to determine when you must start getting ready. Of course, everyone knows that—but most people don't practice it. If you make an honest effort at calculating how long it will take to get dressed for a black-tie event and how long you must allow for transportation to the affair, chances are the amount of time will surprise you! Start calculating your math each day, and you'll begin to find it easier to be on time. Paper and pencil will help in the beginning.

5. Eliminate distractions. "But I started getting ready at seven, and I still can't be out of the door at eight!" reports a client. Chances are, she's getting bogged down by distractions. The phone rings, she stops to listen to the weather report, she takes a "minute" to call a neighbor to offer to do an errand for her. Whether it's getting out of the house in the morning or leaving the office for a meeting, once the time has come that you need to get ready, you need to focus clearly on your departure. At home, put on an answering machine to screen calls; at the office, put on voice mail or ask your secretary to hold calls. Turn off the television and remain focused. You *can* get there on time if you are intent on your on-time goal.

6. Allow for the unexpected. Murphy's law—"If something can go wrong, it will"—comes true almost every day of our lives. In the morning, milk spills, the dog is too busy chasing a squirrel to come in when you need him to, it's raining so now boots and umbrellas must be found—the list of possibilities is endless. At work, an urgent call comes through just before you need to leave for a meeting. At the last minute you can't locate some new statistics someone called and asked you to bring. The phone keeps on ringing, a co-worker has a question, the temporary worker wants you to sign some letters. You're never going to get out of the office on time. The solution, of course, is to plan for the unexpected. There are two ways to do this:

- Anticipate as much as you can. Look ahead at your week and evaluate whether your schedule holds any trouble spots that should be smoothed out before they cause chaos. If you're expecting out-of-town guests to visit for a few nights, stock up on extra food. If you've asked a temporary worker to prepare letters for you to sign, check with her ten minutes before your departure. If she's got them ready, you can sign them while you still have time.

- Allow extra time. Anyone with a family should allow fifteen extra minutes in the morning for the unexpected. Someone alone may need only an extra five to ten minutes to allow for distractions such as an unexpected phone call you need to take or changing a tie that doesn't look right. At the office, having a ten-minute buffer between the time you intend to leave and the time you really need to leave will stand you in good stead.

MASTERING THE LATE APPOINTMENT DILEMMA

Like on-time airplanes, on-time appointments help keep us sane. To decrease the likelihood of wasting time waiting, try the following:

- Ask for the first appointment of the day. Doctors, dentists, and businesspeople frequently lose "a few minutes" as the day goes by, and they are more likely to be on time early in the day.

- When you note an appointment in your planner, write down the telephone number, address, and directions for getting there (if needed). This way you'll be on time and can confirm that the person you're meeting intends to be on time, too.

- Confirm your appointment the day before. That way if there has been any change in scheduling, you'll know about it in advance.

- If you have a midday medical appointment, call ahead to ask if the doctor is running on time. If he or she is running late, you can get a better estimate as to the time you'll actually get into the examining room.

Morning Management

A good start to the day is a great step forward in the battle against feeling overwhelmed. To get out of the house on time, morning planning starts the night before.

Do as Much as You Can the Night Before

- Select your clothing. Check to be certain that everything is in good condition—no loose buttons or scuffed shoes. (If you make it a policy never to put away anything that needs to be laundered, mended, or ironed, you won't find any surprises.) Listen to the weather report so that your selections will be appropriate.

- If you have children, choose their clothing or help them make the selection themselves.

- Run the dishwasher right after dinner and empty it later that night. Set the breakfast table so that the only kitchen chores for morning are breakfast-related ones.

- If any family members take lunches, prepare them the night before.

- Briefcases, purses, and backpacks (which should be each child's responsibility) should all be packed up the night before. Lay them out by the door.

- On a hall table near where you exit, lay out any additional items you'll need: gloves, umbrella, tote bag, and make sure your wallet contains your commuter pass and/or parking meter change, etc.

- Do you have errands to run while you're out? Lay out shoes that need to go to the shoemaker, library books, items to be returned to the store, etc.

- Leave a checklist on the kitchen counter for anything you might forget in the morning. You need to confirm an appointment and weren't able to reach the person yesterday. You've had to refrigerate a casserole you're dropping off for an ill neighbor. Johnny needs to check and record his home barometer reading for his science project, etc. Anything unusual that needs to be taken care of in the morning should be noted on this checklist.

- Children can use checklists, too. Make a check-off chart for what each child is responsible for in the morning (get dressed, brush teeth, make bed, take out trash), and teach them to check each item off as it's accomplished.

Develop a System for the Morning

- If you're a parent, have a standing backup plan for child care. ("I can't come in today," uttered by any child-care person, are five words that send chills up the spine of all working parents.) Whether it's asking a relative to come in, dropping the kids at the neighbors, or calling an agency to send over a temporary worker, have in mind what you will do if your child-care coverage falls through.

- Make certain you have clocks that are easily visible in the rooms where you get ready. (Few people have clocks in the bathroom, yet this is where a great amount of preparation time takes place.) By keeping track of whether or not you're on schedule, you'll find it much easier to be on time.

- Is bathroom time a problem at your house? Then call a family meeting to set up a schedule and coordinate times. Grooming activities such as use of a hair dryer might be moved to the bedroom to allow other family members access to the bathroom.

- Make your bed as soon as you get up.

- If you have young children, get yourself dressed first. It's easier to manage the children if you're already prepared.

- Move through the house methodically so that you don't lose time running from room to room as you get ready. If you have a toddler to dress, help him or her into the pre-selected clothes and work together to make the bed so that as you leave that room, you have no reason you need to go back.

- Limit children's breakfast choices, and be certain that they're dressed and have eaten before they are given permission to play or watch television.

- Employ family teamwork to get everyone ready, such as asking family members to put their own dishes in the dishwasher. (Even a kindergartner can do this.)

- Use an answering machine to screen morning calls. Although you do want to receive the call that cancels your morning dental appointment, you don't want to get caught with a long-winded neighbor whom you can talk to later in the day.

- Plan for appropriate travel delays. If your route is subject to bad traffic, always plan for the worst. That way you needn't be anxious while waiting for the traffic to move.

- If you're leaving with children (or even your spouse), provide warnings: "Ten minutes until we need to go," or "We need to leave in five minutes." That way everyone knows the schedule. With children, add reminder tasks: "Ten minutes to go. Are your shoes on?" "Have you brushed your teeth?"

- If you find that you're running late, keep asking yourself: "What must be done now, and what must wait?" (You must get dressed; bed making can wait.) Keep asking this until you're out the door.

CREATING THE RIGHT ENVIRONMENT

Part of good time management is operating in an environment that works for you—where you can find what you need when you need it. By addressing little chores (bed making, morning dishes, rehanging towels, laundry in hamper) as they arise, there's no catching up to do when you get home.

For the Chronically Late

- Set your clocks and watch a few minutes ahead.

- Write down appointments in your calendar for earlier than they really are. A 10:15 A.M. dental appointment should be put down for 10:00 A.M.

- Tell family members who dawdle that they must be prepared earlier than they really need to be.

- Set a kitchen timer for fifteen-minute time intervals. The timer will help you keep track of how quickly time is passing.

■ Streamline everything: what you wear (limit color choices and select a few outfits that work together); how you "dress" your bed (try a comforter with a duvet cover and eliminate top sheets and fancy pillows); set coffee timer for the night before; eat yogurt, which is faster and healthier than pancakes; spring for buying lunch several times a week to eliminate having to fix it. Treat yourself to a professionally "blown-out" hair style once a week; it will save you a few minutes for several mornings.

■ If you live alone, use a buddy system. Ask someone to phone to get you up. One client even made an agreement to walk to the subway with his neighbor so that he knew that he had to be ready to leave on time. If you drive to work, a carpool could accomplish this, too.

Checkpoint and Review

Are You Getting More Places on Time?
To reform a bad habit like being late, you need to remember the following:

1. Make promptness a priority.
If it was important enough for you to agree to, then it's important enough for you to arrange to get there on time.

2. Maintain control of your time.
Resist answering the phone as you dash out the door; don't relax for "five more minutes with the paper" in the morning. Your day will be better if your travel time isn't haunted by the thought of being late. If you have a few extra minutes upon arrival, you can relax then.

3. Remember the principles of promptness:

- **Plan ahead.**

  - What do you need to do in advance?

  - What do you need to take with you?

- **Create an orderly environment.**

  - Establish permanent places for items such as keys, coats, and outdoor accessories.

  - Stipulate a place near the door where family members can lay out what they'll need for their departures.

  - At the office, establish files or use your briefcase to put papers you'll need for an out-of-office meeting.

- **Establish helpful routines.**

  - For regular departures such as leaving for school or work, set up a routine that you follow habitually. If you're eating breakfast at 7:40 instead of 7:30, you will already know that you're running a little late and need to make up the lost time.

- **Determine at what time you need to begin getting ready.** Do your math! Add preparation time to travel time to decide what hour you need to begin getting ready.

- **Eliminate distractions.** Screen phone calls and keep your mind on staying on schedule.

- **Allow for the unexpected.**

  - Anticipate any problems you can.

  - Add an extra ten to fifteen minutes to allow for delays in your departure.

4. To streamline your morning departure:

- Do as much as you can the night before. Don't wait until the morning crunch to do chores that can easily fit into your evening schedule.

- Practice good morning management. Develop a system and employ family team work to get out of the house on time.

CHAPTER 11

· · · · · · · ·

Time-Management Emergencies: Coping with the Unexpected

Unfortunately, time-management emergencies happen all the time. Read through the following list and check off those unexpected events you've experienced within the last month:

_____ You or one of your children had to stay home sick, necessitating that you make special arrangements.

_____ A special project came up at work, and your boss ordered you to bump all other work in order to make this a priority.

_____ You misplaced something and had to turn the house (or your office) upside down trying to find it.

_____ Another person cancelled an appointment that was important to you.

_____ Someone else promised they'd help you with something (drive the carpool, fill in for you with a volunteer organization), and they called to back out.

_____ You were supposed to pick up something at a store that was ready and waiting for you, but when you got there they couldn't find it.

_____ You were stuck in traffic that delayed you for more than fifteen minutes.

_____ You were kept waiting for an appointment with a doctor or dentist.

When something occurs that we don't expect, it puts our day off schedule and, depending on the circumstances, sometimes throws us completely out of control.

The unexpected happens so frequently that we ought to learn to expect it—that's what a good time manager does. He or she anticipates that something may go wrong with the best-laid plans and has already considered how to handle it. And therein, of course, lies the secret: managing the unexpected so that you can get back in control. The sooner you can do this, the more rapidly you can take care of the emergency as well as anything that was delayed because of the crisis.

This chapter is brief—as befits anything written about an emergency—but it provides you with a strategy about how to cope when the unexpected occurs:

Anticipating the unexpected
Managing the unanticipated
Post-emergency management

Anticipating the Unexpected

Although there is no way to predict certain unexpected occurrences (a traffic jam that makes you late for an appointment or a job interview that was moved to an earlier hour to suit the interviewer's schedule), some emergencies can actually be planned on. Consider these examples:

- Your car has been making lots of strange noises. If you ignore them, you can wake up one morning to discover that it no longer starts.

- At work, you've increased the responsibilities for a new employee, and he hasn't really been managing that well. Some bosses would ignore the signals and be caught blind-sided when something important goes wrong. The smart boss (and time manager) will begin to observe what is happening and calculate how he or she wants to cope with it (closer supervision? ultimate replacement?).

■ Or one of your kids just hasn't been herself. While she may have had no fever or specific symptoms, it shouldn't be a total surprise when you hear from the school nurse that you need to take her home.

In each of these cases, there were signals that something was going wrong. If the car is taken to a mechanic before it breaks down, that crisis is averted. If you know an employee is in over his head, you, or someone you appoint, needs to double-check his work so that nothing cataclysmic occurs. And if you know that a sick child is a possibility, you'll begin to bring work home or figure out strategies of who could stay home with her if you can't.

The more time you've had to mull over solutions, the greater the likelihood that you'll manage the unexpected with ease.

> ### *The best way to handle an emergency is by preventing it.*

Managing the Unanticipated

Many events that occur cannot be anticipated (delays and cancellations caused by people you don't know well can rarely be foreseen), and it's impossible to prepare. In situations like these, there are some specific steps you can take in order to maintain control:

1. Think carefully about the emergency, and if someone has brought a problem to you, ask questions to clarify. Consider:

- Is this really my emergency? If you're stuck in traffic, then, yes, but if someone else at work failed to do their job or has come to you with a problem, it may or may not have to affect your day.

- Can I give this emergency to someone else? If it's work that didn't get done, then it may not be your place to fill in. Don't offer unless you're sure you're the only one who can do it.

2. If you decide this unexpected event is indeed your responsibility, then consider how best to manage it.

   - If you're kept waiting for an appointment, can you make good use of the time so that the wait really isn't a problem?

   - Can you delay the emergency? Must it really be handled immediately?

3. Once caught up in the emergency (running late, having to fit something extra into your day), stay in control. Work through whatever must be done, and keep asking: "What's the best use of my time right now? What must get done? What can wait?" It will help you set the moment-to-moment priorities necessary for the occasion.

Post-Emergency Management

Because emergencies tend to throw our plans out of kilter, your first priority once you've managed the unexpected is assessing the damage.

What needs to be done to catch up? If you were able to delegate your work to someone else, then you may be able to move on to the next thing, but if you missed dinner with a friend because of a sick child, you probably want to book something else to do with that person.

Do you owe anyone a thank-you for helping out during the crisis?

Checkpoint and Review

1. Anticipate problems.
If you see them coming, it's easier to prepare.

2. Take charge of the unanticipated.

- Consider various approaches.

- Manage what occurs.

- Keep asking, "What's the best use of my time right now?"

3. Afterward consider:
What do you need to do to catch up?

Section 4

HELPFUL TIME-MANAGEMENT SYSTEMS

CHAPTER 12

. . . .

Errands: Running Them Efficiently So They Don't Run You!

"Errands eat up my life!" declared one client shortly after we began work at her home. "No sooner do I finish one set of them than it seems there are more to do!"

Today's busy pace of life brings with it lots of additional duties—whether it's picking up specialty ingredients for a dinner party, buying fruit at the fresh produce market, dropping off dry cleaning, selecting a frame for a photograph, or purchasing a birthday gift, there is always something on the list of things to do or buy.

When it comes to errands, there are two things you can be sure of: They never go away, and they are never divided fairly among family members!

Because so many families now consist of dual wage earners, some corporations have actually added some helpful perks. They've established a company "concierge," where employees can leave laundry and dry cleaning and shoes for repair; some companies offer a variety of other services as well. The corporations must believe that by lessening the stress on employees during their off hours, the company will gain loyal employees who are better prepared to devote themselves to their work.

Unfortunately, most of us do not yet profit from this type of employee benefit, so we need to develop errand strategies of our own.

Establishing a system for running your errands will provide you with a set schedule and an efficient method for getting these tasks taken care of—no more dragging home with your shopping bags overflowing only to discover you've forgotten something.

This chapter will discuss

- Division of responsibilities

- Establishing a schedule and a system

- What to do when you get home

- When kids are along

- Alternatives to errands

Share Your Responsibilities

In this day and age, couples need to share household and family responsibilities. If you're married and have not already split up some of the errand running, now is the time to do so. There will likely be certain errands that are very convenient for one person and not so easy for the other. Set a time when the two of you can coordinate on the tasks for that week.

Establishing a Schedule

In today's busy world, setting a schedule for doing errands can take you a long way toward making it a less burdensome part of your week. Most of my clients complain that their Saturdays disappear because there are so many errands to do. The solution, of course, is to develop a system that minimizes weekend intrusion. The benefits of a schedule are twofold.

Family members will become accustomed to knowing that their wants will be taken care of at a certain time, and you'll develop a habitual method for taking care of what you need to do.

Consider these options, keeping in mind that avoiding peak periods at any type of store will help you accomplish your chores faster and with less stress:

- Are there shops near your job where you could get some of your errands accomplished? Many working people find that by using one lunch hour per week to buy toiletries, pick up a birthday gift, or even patronize a near-work shoemaker, they can reduce what they need to do on weekends.

- Begin noticing shops near home or office that offer extended hours. You might like to select one evening after work that you could use to take care of a few things. In most communities there are twenty-four-hour super- markets and drugstores, offering customers new options as to when to shop. Many malls are regularly open until eight or nine, and most downtown areas offer late-night shopping once per week. This expands your opportunity to get things done, and on occasions when your errand list is light, you might meet your spouse or a friend for a quick bite to lighten the drudgery of running errands.

- If you have children, it's preferable to leave them at home at times when you're working on a long list of things to do. Perhaps your child-care worker could routinely stay an extra hour on Thursdays, or perhaps your spouse can cover home base one night per week.

- Even if you can't regularly devote a lunch hour or a week- night, you may still find odd moments throughout the week to fit in small tasks (on the way to or from work per- haps). Anything you can do conveniently that reduces your errand load (buy in bulk, shop by mail, patronize stores where you can order by phone and they'll deliver) will be highly beneficial.

- Establish a time period for those items that must be held over for Saturday. (Most people prefer getting errands over with in the morning.) Then be certain that you use the rest of the day for something you enjoy.

Plan Ahead

Planning ahead is the key to avoiding the errand run-around. You know how it goes—you arrive home and realize you forgot something, so sooner or later you've got to run back out, and if you haven't planned ahead, the process just keeps repeating itself. Here's what to do:

Within your master notebook, establish an "Errands" category where you can keep a running list of all that you need to do each week.

- Note down everything from returning library books and dropping off a jacket for the seamstress to alter to stopping to look at new dryers if yours will soon need to be replaced.

- Ask that family members inform you—or leave you a note—if they need something and won't be able to take care of it themselves. "Mom, I need new sneakers" will tell you that you and your child will need to stop at a shoe store this weekend.

- Anticipate. Mother's Day may be six weeks away, meaning that there's no urgency about picking up a gift. However, the sooner you take care of it, the more quickly you can put it out of your mind.

Near the door by which you exit, establish a "way station," a stopping place for the items you need to take with you on your errands: library books (devote a special on-the-go tote for that purpose and load it up as you finish with the books); shoes for repair; merchandise to return (don't forget the necessary receipts); coupon for discount at the hardware store, etc. Throughout the week you can place things on this table, bench, or chair so that you'll have everything organized on errand day. If you have little ones, make sure these items are kept out of reach of tiny hands that grab and misplace, causing you precious minutes of searching for them!

Purchase a carry-all bag to make your shopping easier. I lived in the city for so many years that I favor the very light-weight style that folds up and can be stored in the bottom of a handbag, but many people are quite happy keeping a canvas tote in their car and taking it in with them when they need it.

Before you leave:

- Within your wallet, order your bills by denomination to make it easier to pay for items, especially if you're in a hurry.

- Take along a few coins in case you need change or parking meter money, but don't take so much that it weighs you down.

- Take along tickets or tokens for public transportation if needed.

- Take the credit cards you'll be using and have your checks and check register with you. By having the register along, it eliminates having to enter the checking information when you get home—another thing to do. Be certain to have your driver's license or other forms of identification as well.

- Take your errand list and anything you may need for decision-making (tape measure for checking furniture size; paint chip for matching fabric to wall color; room measurements, photos for which you need frames, etc.).

- Bring a magazine or something to do in case you have waiting time. (If it's going to take a few minutes for the store to pack the lamp you purchased, you're prepared.)

Out and About

Plan your route so that you don't backtrack, keeping in mind that one of your final stops should be any store where you plan to purchase perishables.

When you can, shop in stores that are familiar to you. If you know exactly where the children's socks are, picking up some extra pairs will take only moments of your time.

Whenever you're buying an item you use regularly, buy in bulk. The bigger the quantity, the longer the time before you have to do that errand again.

Buy it when you see it. Even if your son's birthday party is a month away, buy the paper goods with the right motif when you find them. It will save you shopping time later on, and you won't have to worry about whether that design will still be in stock when you need it.

If you're purchasing a gift, ask that it be wrapped. Most stores offer this at no extra charge. If you're buying in advance, attach a small label to it when you get home: "For Jim, electric drill." This will tell you what it is and who you're saving it for.

As you shop, keep track of your receipts. Some people prefer to keep them in the shopping bag to be sorted out at home. I recommend collecting them in the store and immediately putting them in your purse or wallet; it's a time saver. All your receipts are in one place to be filed with your unpaid bills (see the following chapter about bill paying), and you avoid hunting for those pieces of paper in the large shopping bags.

Your Arrival Home

No errand mission is complete until you've come home and put everything away. What good are new razor blades if you can't find them because they never got unpacked? I've visited countless homes where I'll find items left in the bags they came home in buried under papers. Other new purchases will be out of the bag but not unwrapped or put away. Still other items do end up in the closet, but on the floor, still with tag labels on them!

- When you arrive, place all your bags and purchases at the "way station," and take a moment to hang up your coat. Then start unpacking.

- Put away perishables first.

- Now unpack your other bags and sort according to the area of the house. After sorting, you can reuse one of the shopping bags to carry purchases to various parts of the house.

- As you distribute items to the proper areas, take time to unwrap each item, clip tags, and put it away. On the day that you need it, you may be in a hurry. If children bombard you once you come home, enlist their help. If the phone rings, let the machine pick it up until you're settled. If there's a real emergency, handle it first, and then come back to the putting away.

If You Have Children

Errands are easier to do when the children aren't along. However, there are often occasions when it makes sense to take them:

- There's no one at home with whom they can stay.

- You need them along to check sizes or for them to make a selection.

- Some children actually enjoy doing errands with you, and if they are age six or older, it's often a fun time to have them along.

If you'll have them with you, here are some things to keep in mind:

- Be certain they've just had a snack, a drink of water, and have gone to the bathroom before you leave. You'll never get anything accomplished if you have to worry about these things right away!

- If you're taking a baby or toddler, use a stroller or some type of carrying device that leaves your hands free but keeps the child with you at all times.

- Take along a bag of appropriate amusements and small snacks: a bottle and a rattle for a baby; a bag of dry cereal and a toy for a toddler; a coloring or reading book for an older child.

- Give your child a job. A preschooler can be in charge of carrying something for brief periods of time. Children who can read can be put in charge of the list.

- Plan the expedition so that there's a reward at the end. Can one of your final errands be near an ice cream store? A shared treat with a parent can make any boring errand excursion worthwhile.

Alternatives to Errand Running

Since so many people feel overwhelmed about all the things they need to do, the ultimate in time management is to reduce the number of errands that take up your time. Here are some alternatives:

- Shop by mail order.

- Patronize businesses that deliver.

- Consider placing standing orders. From pet supplies and groceries to the newspaper, having a regular delivery can save you both the planning and errand time.

- Use local shops, but order by phone. They may deliver, or once the order is ready you can pick it up.

- Investigate all services that will come to you. In many places there are dog groomers, personal trainers, hair stylists, and other service providers who are ready to travel.

- If you have children over age twelve, they may be able to help with errands. Could they walk to a nearby store? If not, take them with you and divide responsibilities, meeting up at one of the area stores.

- Hire teens to help out, or use special shopping services. With so many people working today, you can actually hire special services to take care of anything from corporate gift buying to getting your car to the service station for repair. Check the classified ads or ask around.

Checkpoint and Review

1. Divide responsibilities with your spouse.

- Discuss it weekly.
- Share according to individual convenience.

2. Establish a schedule. Consider alternatives to Saturday.

- Do errands on your lunch hour.
- Select an evening after work.

3. Plan ahead.

- Keep an ongoing list; get input from family members.
- Establish a "way station" near your door so that you can lay out items for your next errand trip.
- Get organized before you leave. Take the list, a few coins, cash, personal checkbook, driver's license or other ID, ticket or tokens for public transport (if needed), and something to do.

4. On your errands:

- Plan a convenient route that makes sense—no backtracking.

- Shop at familiar stores.

- Buy in bulk.

- Buy it when you see it.

5. Once home:

- Unpack everything!

- Clip tags and put away.

6. If you have kids along:

- Feed them a snack and have them go to the bathroom before departure.

- With little ones, put them in a stroller or other carrier that keeps them with you but leaves your hands free.

- Take along food and age-appropriate amusements.

- Let them be in charge of some aspect of the expedition.

- Plan a reward for the end.

7. Consider alternatives to errand running.

- Shop by mail.

- Patronize stores that deliver.

- Consider placing standing orders.

- Buy from local stores but shop by phone.

- Investigate services that will come to you.

- Are your children over twelve? Ask them to help.

- Hire teens or shopping services to help get things off your list.

CHAPTER 13

. . . .

Banking and Bill Paying

When it comes to banking and bill paying, are you ever guilty of the following:

YES   NO

_____   _____   I usually don't bother to reconcile my bank statement. I figure they know what they're doing.

_____   _____   I write a check at a doctor's office and by the time I get home to enter it into my check register, I've forgotten the check number and amount!

_____   _____   I sometimes leave the bills with other unopened mail, and at the first of the month I can't always find the invoices.

_____   _____   I never save my store receipts, so they could charge me for something extra, and I'd never know.

_____   _____   I don't really have a system. I pay some bills when they come in, and others I just set aside for when I have time.

_____ _____ I'd like to know more about electronic bill
paying, but I'm afraid it won't work for me.
_____ _____ When it comes to bill paying, I procrastinate!

Banking and bill paying—two of life's more tedious tasks!
Everyone likes what money buys; no one likes having to keep a
record of it.

So much depends on knowing the state of your finances that
it's vital to have an efficient way of getting the job done so that
you can easily keep track of income and out-go. If you had
even one yes in the above quiz, this chapter will help by
showing you how to:

- Better manage your banking time
- Keep an up-to-date checkbook
- Establish a system and a schedule for bill paying
- Computerize your finances
- Investigate online banking and bill paying

At the Bank

Remember the days when people used to stand in long lines
on payday in order to deposit their paychecks? Those days are
disappearing because so many companies now offer employees
the option of having paychecks directly deposited in their
bank accounts. No more lines, no more worrying about how to
get your paycheck if you're away or sick on the day you're paid.
If you're not benefiting from this option, check with your
employer, and sign up now. It's a definite time saver.

However, despite direct deposits and other advances like
ATM's, drive-through windows, and electronic banking, there
will always be times when we must visit a bank, so it's worth the
time to select a user-friendly one. If you're changing banks,
consider both their financial products as well as their devotion

to service. Are there long lines for anything—to speak to an officer? at a teller's window? at the ATM machine? Are there evening or Saturday hours? If a bank hasn't streamlined its service capabilities, this isn't the bank for you.

When you do have banking to do, here's how to best manage your time:

- Get to know one bank officer, and let her get to know you. Building a relationship will assure you of better banking for many years.

- Visit the bank during periods of least activity. Lunch hours and early Monday and late Friday are still the most heavily trafficked times at most banks.

- Before going to the bank, have everything (deposit and withdrawal slips, check endorsements) ready so that you can be in and out quickly. (And just in case there's a line, have something with you to read.)

- When opening an account for yourself or your children, call ahead to find out about any documentation you'll need (Social Security number, proof of residency, etc.) so that you'll only need to visit the bank once to get the task accomplished.

- Whenever possible, use the ATM machine. It's generally quicker and easier.

- If you're fourth or fifth on line at the drive-up window, turn around, park your car, and go into the bank instead. It will definitely save you time.

The Traditional Checkbook

Though electronic banking and bill paying is becoming an established and growing method of managing family finances, most people still prefer their good old checkbook. If you're making a continuing commitment to a paper-based system, get in the habit of keeping an accurate, well-maintained one. You'll know where you stand financially, and because you're aware of what's going on in your account, you'll notice if the bank makes an error.

Long-term record keeping is important, so start by purchasing a cancelled-checks folder for each bank account. Label each folder with the account number and the current year. The folder is sectioned off by month, and this is where you'll keep your bank statements after you've reconciled them.

Order a desk-style checkbook. These books make for easier record keeping since there is ample room to note details. Also order a portable checkbook (the ones that are the exact size of the check). Keep reading to learn why.

Record every check and every deposit. This is an easy task if you keep up with it, but too many of my clients entrust their record keeping to the bank, leaving them powerless to discover an error in their own account. If you have not been in the habit of keeping your checkbook up to date, now is the time to reform. Here are three ways to do it:

1. Always request a receipt for deposits and ATM transactions. When you arrive home, make a habit of noting your deposit or withdrawal in your checkbook. Next, file your receipt in the current-month section of your cancelled-check folder until your bank statement arrives. Note the source of all deposits so that you'll have a permanent record of what money was income and what was from other sources.

2. Remember the small checkbook you ordered? It's for writing checks when you're away from home. When you write a check at the dentist or a department store, you record the check in the small checkbook you have with you. This is far more efficient than noting the check number and amount on a scrap of paper the way most people do. When you get home, it's easy to transfer the information to your desk register.

3. At the end of every bill-paying session, make certain that you have recorded every check, noted the amount, and calculated your new balance.

YOUR CHECKBOOK: KEEPING IT STRAIGHT

When your bank statement arrives, reconcile it right away. For every day that passes, there will be more and more transactions, making the reconciliation even more time-consuming.

As you compare statement to check register, check off those that have come through. Circle any entries that have not yet cleared to make your work the following month that much easier.

Once completed, file the statement in your cancelled-checks folder.

Bill Paying: Establishing a System

Buy a household-affairs folder at a local stationery store to use for storing bills, both paid and unpaid. These are oversize accordion folders that are separated into many sections and labeled by month or category: Automobile, Bank, Income Taxes, Insurance, Medical, Real Estate, Receipts, Rent/Mortgage, Utilities, and a separate slot for Unpaid Bills. Label the folder with the current year. (If you're starting this project mid-year, collect your paid bills from earlier in the year and file them by category or by month, depending on the style of folder you selected.)

To begin, simplify your bill-paying chore by limiting the number of charge cards you use. Major bank cards are now accepted almost everywhere, and the fewer the cards you use, the fewer bills you have to pay.

All store receipts should be filed in the Unpaid Bills section of the folder until the appropriate bill arrives. When you make a purchase, take the receipt from the clerk and put it in your wallet or a separate envelope you carry for that purpose. This will make filing them at home a simpler process.

When bills arrive in the mail, pull them immediately. Open the envelope and take a quick look to be certain that the account seems to be in good order. Cross-check the invoices against store receipts now. Don't wait until it's time to pay the bill.

If you are concerned about any of the amounts on the bill, double-check with family members about anything they may have charged. If you still feel there is a problem, contact the store or company to discuss making corrections to your account immediately.

If nothing concerns you, toss any advertising mailers that have come with the bill and put everything back in the envelope for safekeeping until bill-paying day. Mark on the exterior of the envelope the bill's due date and file it under Unpaid Bills.

Solicitations for donations from organizations that interest you should be filed with unpaid bills. After you've paid out what you owe, you'll be prepared to decide what to give.

Who Pays the Bills?

Household bills. One person in the family should be responsible for all major bills (rent or mortgage, utilities, medical bills, etc.). This eliminates confusion and guess work, duplicate payments or no payment at all. Some families like to rotate this job every six months so that both husband and wife have a good idea of what's happening with the family's finances.

Credit card and department store bills. Other bills could be taken care of by the family-appointed "bill payer" or paid by the person primarily responsible for incurring the charges. For example, a husband and wife may each want to pay their own charge card bills or be responsible for a specific department store bill.

Dividing by usage is a good time saver because if it's your

credit card bill, most of the charges will be familiar to you, which helps in assessing the bill's accuracy. Many couples prefer this system, too, because in many cases the payments will be written on their personal checking account rather than a joint one. (This also permits you to gift shop for a spouse without revealing what something cost.) How to remember which you pay? If the bill is addressed to you, it's yours.

Establish a Schedule

A twice-a-month bill-paying schedule makes sense from a time-management standpoint. It's often enough to be on time but not so often that it becomes burdensome. From a financial standpoint, bills can be paid closer to when they are due, and your bank account can take a breather between assaults on the balance.

When you pay your bills, have on hand:

- Your household-affairs folder with unpaid bills and store receipts in the file

- cancelled-checks folder

- pen

- note paper

- checkbook

- calculator or adding machine

- extra envelopes

- return-address embosser or labels

- stamps

- wastebasket

If you didn't have time to do it before, examine each bill and compare store receipts to charges. If you're satisfied that the bill is accurate, write the check for the proper amount, and note your account number (or other form of appropriate identification) on the front of the check.

Enter the amount paid in your check register and also note any additional helpful information: Place a check in the Tax column if the item is deductible; note for which month you are paying the music teacher; or if you have more than one phone line and they are billed separately, write down for which line you are paying with this check.

Put your check and the correct portion of the invoice into the provided envelope (be sure the address shows through the envelope window). If the bill you just paid isn't due right away, estimate when to mail it in order for it to arrive on time. Note the date by the stamp on the envelope and wait to mail it on that day.

Mark your portion of the invoice "paid" and note the date, amount, and check number (a time saver if you later encounter questions about whether a payment was made). Then file it by category (Automobile for car payment, Utilities for the electric bill) or by month.

Any receipt concerning the purchase of your home or for a home improvement should be saved until you've sold the home, so these receipts should be moved into a permanent file. After paying bills of this sort, remove the receipts (mark them paid and note the date and check number) and file them in a House file in your file cabinet (see Chapter 15).

Once all bills have been paid, take out any solicitations you've received. Would you like to give money to any of the organizations? If so, now is the time. Keep a list of organizations to which you've given money, noting the date. This provides you with a means of checking that your annual membership really is due at this time.

Before closing your checkbook, be certain to calculate your new balance.

Let Your Bank Do the Work

Automatic fund transfers are an easy way to let your bank take care of recurring payments that are unvarying in amount and due date (like your mortgage or insurance payments). This has nothing to do with personal computers or online banking. All you need to do is contact your bank to arrange for them to automatically transfer the money to the other institution.

This type of "standing order" is also a great system for savings. Leave instructions with the bank as to how much money should go directly to your savings account or brokerage firm, and that way the money won't even be there to tempt you.

Or have you considered banking by phone? If you don't have a personal computer with modem pickup, you might explore this option. With only a phone call you can

- Make balance inquiries

- Verify deposits and confirm checks paid out

- Get a summary of transactions

- Stop payment on a check

- Pay bills by phone

Inquire at your local bank.

Personal Finances on Computer

When it comes to money management, the greatest time saver ever invented lies within personal finance software for your computer. Tasks like budgeting, tracking expenses, or organizing figures for the IRS that used to take a lot of time and require a great deal of paper can now be done with the stroke of a few computer keys. All it takes is selecting the software that is right for your needs and entering your figures on a regular basis. (If you keep up with it, entering the information takes only a few minutes per week.)

- Talk to friends and read reviews in computer and financial magazines to select the financial program that's best for you. (Read the section concerning electronic bill paying later in this chapter for additional insight into selecting a software program.)

- Once the program is installed and you've become familiar with it, you'll find that it's very helpful. If you want to know how much you've donated and to which organizations, you can find out in no time. Do you want to know what damage you did to your savings on your recent vacation? And what about finding out whether or not a bill was paid or totaling up family income for the year? That information will be there.

- Some people actually use these programs (some of which have check-writing capabilities) instead of their checkbook, making data entry a single activity: the check is written by the computer and the dollars involved are categorized automatically.

- If you have a modem, you can also regularly monitor your investments.

- Because your financial information is already organized and easily accessible, you may also find that you'll pay less for tax preparation because you're so well prepared.

Online Banking

Soon we'll all have up-to-the-minute access to the status of our bank account simply by dialing in from our home computer. Some people are already beginning to enjoy this luxury through online services and through their own banks as well as a few banks that have opened "virtual branches" in cyberspace.

What It Does. These at-home banking services make it easy to download bank transactions, transfer funds, automatically reconcile checkbooks, and pay bills online using just your PC and modem. Some services are also beginning to offer the opportunity for you to review your credit card account, and some have facilities for you to buy and sell stock as well.

What You'll Pay. So far it's quite affordable. Because banks want customers to switch (the banks are envisioning cost savings through the closings of local branches as more and more people bank online), they're keeping fees low and providing twenty-four-hour customer telephone support in order to encourage the transition. If your bank is not yet offering online services, you can still pay checks electronically by using money-management software and using a bill-payment service. Competition is keeping fees at these services low, too. Investigate current prices and see—the per-check charge may not be much more than what you're currently investing in postage.

Who Likes It. This new style of banking is becoming particularly popular with people who are already using personal finance software and with frequent travelers, who enjoy the convenience of being able to pay bills while they are gone and who can use a laptop computer and modem hookup to check on their accounts. It's also a great help for those managing the finances of an elderly relative.

If you're interested in online banking, you'll need a computer and a modem. Then you're ready to select between two basic types of services:

1. Some services function as an at-home ATM machine with bill-paying capabilities (though you'll never be able to make a deposit or get it to spew out cash from the wall!). You can see account information, make transfers between accounts, and pay bills. These services are usually offered through banks, and to operate them you generally need to obtain the bank's proprietary software (sometimes given free).

2. Some services are accessible because you're using a specific type of personal money-management software. The advantage to these systems is that it categorizes and tracks

your spending when you conduct your basic banking business—no additional work on your part. The disadvantage is that if your bank does not offer an interface with the software you've selected, you must sign up with a special bill-payment company in order to transfer money and pay your bills. (Keep reading for more information on these services.) There is generally a twelve- to twenty-four-hour lag time between any banking transaction you perform (paying a bill, withdrawing cash, which you still have to do at a bank or an ATM machine) and seeing it on your computer screen because of the delay in running the data through this third-party bill-payment system.

Electronic Bill Paying

Electronic bill paying is an additional option available through online banking. It relieves you of the tedium of writing checks, stuffing envelopes, and getting the bills mailed by the correct date.

To get started, you need to complete a simple application form, choose a personal identification number, and send in a voided printed check for verification. You will receive an account number and a local modem-access number to use for transmitting payments. These will be your permanent tools for bill paying.

When you're ready to make a payment, you do it all on your computer, and you'll find that it's easy to do—software makers have designed it so that it's much like writing out a real check. For your first session you'll provide the payee, the address, your account number, and the amount you're paying. The bill-paying service will transfer the money electronically, and your payment will show up on your bank statement (remember, though, you'll no longer have the documentation of a cancelled check). If a company to whom you owe money does not accept electronic payments, your service will take care of preparing and mailing a real check.

At subsequent bill-paying sessions, the address and account information on the regular bills you pay will already be on file in your computer program, so you'll need only to enter the new amount owed and the date on which you want the money sent—you'll be saving check-writing time every month.

This system offers the ultimate in control. When you pay electronically, merchants receive money on the day you specify; funds clear your account on the day you expect; your electronic checking account is automatically balanced by the computer; and your expenses are categorized automatically, all through the push of a key.

Another advantage to this system is better use of your money, particularly if your funds are in an interest-bearing account. You can keep the money in your account for as long as is reasonable, and then let it go to the payee. (Experience shows that you need to allow "processing" time, from two to six business days, so don't try transferring funds on the day that your bill is due.)

SECURITY AND RELIABILITY?

When it comes to cyberspace, there are always concerns about security, but at this point there is no cause for major concern for home bankers. Banks are keenly aware of this issue, and unless you have given out your personal identification number (PIN), federal law makes unauthorized use of your account the bank's liability, not yours.

These businesses are in their infancy, and perhaps a more logical concern is reliability of the bill-paying aspect of the services. When you opt to try electronic bill paying, find out about the track record of your home-banking service. Some are proving to be more reliable than others, and though most companies promise to resolve any problems and cover any late fees, it's a time waster to have to deal with any type of inefficiency.

With the staggering growth in technology, the world of home banking and money management is improving constantly and ultimately the systems are going to become easier and easier to use. Remain alert to updates because at some point you'll want to take advantage of the great time savings offered through these changes.

Checkpoint and Review

1. Save time when banking by taking the following steps:

- Arrange for direct deposit of your paycheck.

- Select a bank that is "user-friendly."

- When you do need to stop by the bank, go during off hours, and have everything ready to speed the process.

2. Be diligent in managing your checkbook.

- Purchase a cancelled-checks folder, and order a desk-style checkbook as well as a portable checkbook.

- For better account management, get in the habit of recording every transaction.

- Reconcile your checkbook as soon as your bank statement arrives.

3. Establish a system, set a schedule, and appoint one family member to take care of the major household bill paying.

- Buy a household affairs folder for storing both paid and unpaid bills as well as store receipts.

- File solicitations that interest you along with your unpaid bills.

- Schedule two bill-paying sessions per month.

- After bills have been paid, mark the customer portion of the bill "paid" and file it in your household affairs folder or in your permanent files.

4. Leave a standing order with the bank to make fixed payments for you (such as your mortgage payments or transferring funds to savings) via automatic funds transfer.

5. Save time by getting your personal finances on computer. After a small time investment in setting it up, you'll have access to all your financial information with the stroke of a few keys.

6. Online banking is the way of the future; so far banks are keeping fees low and providing round-the-clock access to support personnel in order to encourage people to make the transition. With a computer and a modem you can:

- Gain access to the status of your account and make account transfers twenty-four hours per day.

- With some services, monitor investments.

- Pay bills electronically.

CHAPTER 14

. . . .

The Mail

If you were to ask me, "What can I do to better manage my time?" I would reply: "Learn to manage your mail, because good paper management is your best defense against poor time management."

If you're not managing it very well right now, you're not alone. In the course of my work I've seen some unique systems for mail management:

One woman just never seemed to get around to facing her mail, and she put it wherever there was room—tables, counters, the floor, the couch. The only problem was it got to the point where there was nowhere to sit down.

An executive worked with what he called "My Two Box System." Under his desk were the boxes in question as well as a wastebasket. As he went through his mail, he sorted: "Tossables or Saveables." Into one of the boxes he put letters and memos he thought he might need to hold on to; when one box was filled, he moved the second box forward and filled it. If ever he needed anything, he simply sifted through the boxes, and since items were placed in order of arrival, he claimed it wasn't as difficult as it seemed. Once the second box became filled, the items in the first box were dumped into the trash: "If I haven't needed a paper from there by now, I never will," he explained.

I've also seen countless homes and offices that had no system for the mail—desks and tables and credenzas piled high with the stuff! One woman had saved for so long that she had to create pathways through her papers. It was a mess.

To avoid falling into the traps these people did, you need to look at mail management in a new light.

There was a time when *reading your mail* was an appropriate term. There was much less mail, and what was delivered—personal letters and such—were, indeed, written to be read. Today's mail is different; it's really there to be *managed*. Personal communication is generally done by telephone (or, particularly at the office, by fax or e-mail), so our "home" mail is more likely to consist of bills, invitations, solicitations, magazines, and a back-breaking supply of catalogs. Office mail may include meeting notices, announcements, reports, invitations, job-seeker résumés, professional journals, magazines, and additional miscellany, all of which adds up to a lot.

In this chapter we will discuss mail management for home and office with the following in mind:

- The "where"
- The "when"
- The "how"

Where

Work at your desk, or choose a clear counter or table to go through your mail. Some people actually prefer to stand to do the mail; they find they make quicker decisions and dispose of things more rapidly.

Choose a convenient location for mail sorting, and have on hand:

- A letter opener

- A pen

- A highlighter for marking important sections of letters, reports, or other reading matter

- A small pad of adhesive-backed paper so that you can attach notes for others or reminders to yourself

Nearby you will need:

- a wastebasket

- a recycling bin

When

Despite its importance, mail management is not a prime-time activity. (Your prime time should be saved for more creative work or for thought-oriented tasks.) No matter what time the mail is delivered, *you* should take charge of when it is managed. Here are some guidelines:

- Select an appropriate block of time to go through the mail.

  - At the office, many people like to do the majority of their mail management right before or after lunch.

  - Home mail generally requires a five-to-fifteen-minute block of time. Choose a time when you'll have a minimum of interruptions and can process it in one sitting.

- At the outset, acknowledge your goal: *To sort through the entire pile, tossing or taking care of as much as you can.*

How—Home

If your stack of mail involves items for other family members, sort through all the mail, putting each item in a pile for the appropriate individual.

Each person's mail should then be placed in a specific location. Some households use an entry table with a separate basket for each family member; other families like to take mail directly to children's bedrooms or to a spouse's desk. Choose your method and be consistent.

Now take your own stack of mail and sort through it quickly. Certain items can be tossed (recycled) without even being opened, and toss all those items *now*. This shrinks most piles by almost half.

Now go through your mail one last time, slowly. Open and evaluate everything. By the time you finish this process, you should know exactly what you're doing with each piece of mail. Here are some examples.

Bills

Open each invoice and take a quick look at it. Does the amount due seem right? Compare receipts to invoice now, and if there is a problem you'll want to begin your investigation sooner rather than later. Telephone bills should be read thoroughly on opening. Your memory of whether anyone would have called Tallahassee will be fresher, and if you want to ask if another family member did, indeed, place the call, you should do so now rather than waiting until payment is due.

On all bills, circle the due date and toss all insert materials, saving the invoice and the return envelope. Place these back in the original envelope and mark the due date on the front. You'll need a special folder for Unpaid Bills, and all incoming bills should be filed here. File bills chronologically according to date due. Pay them only once or twice a month. (See Chapter 13 for more information on bill paying.)

Change-of-Address Card and Appointment Reminders

On change-of-address cards, note the change in your address book or roll file, and toss the card.

With appointment reminders, make the call right then and note the appointment date and time on your calendar. If you're sorting the mail in the evening, then put it in your to-do file for tomorrow. If the appointment is for someone else, such as an orthodontic appointment for your youngster, leave a note for him or her and mark it in your calendar and the family wall calendar.

Invitations

Respond immediately. If it's a yes, note it on your calendar and toss the invitation. (If there are directions you'll need, post them on a bulletin board or in your tickler file. See Chapter 16.)

If you need to consult another family member, leave it with their mail with a note attached, asking that they respond by discussing it with you.

Solicitations

Toss those that don't interest you at all, and file other solicitations with your bills. No matter how wonderful the cause, it is more efficient to donate money when you're sending out checks anyway. You can evaluate how generous you feel based on your bank balance after paying the bills.

Catalogs

Shopping by mail can be a major time saver, but the incoming deluge must be managed.

Immediately toss all catalogs that are unappealing or inappropriate for your needs; a quick glance at the first two or three pages will tell you. For instance, if you've just placed an order for pet supplies, toss all incoming pet-related catalogs for a time.

Catalogs you enjoy make great bedtime or on-the-go "reading," and can be saved for this purpose, or you can choose to skim through your favorites right away. Use the smallest size of adhesive-backed note pads (1″ × 1″) to mark pages with items you like, and circle or highlight the item in question. When you refer again to the catalog, you'll know right away what interested you. Toss catalogs that weren't as good as you expected, and establish a place (a file? a shelf?) for catalogs from which you plan to order.

Be a savvy shopper and delay your purchase until you've had the opportunity to compare prices among catalogs; it will still save time over going from store to store. Towels in one catalog may prove less costly than similar ones in another catalog. You'll also find that by delaying you'll save money by cutting down on impulse purchases.

Magazines

Most magazines can be saved to be enjoyed later.

Put work-related magazines directly into your briefcase or near your desk. Magazines you read for pleasure might go in a magazine rack in the living room or on your nightstand. Magazines that arrive unsolicited (some local magazines or those you receive because of a membership) you may decide to toss upon arrival or thumb through quickly to check ads.

The key to getting through your magazines is setting aside time to read them. If you commute by public transportation, you have reading time built into your schedule, so plan to use it. Some people do business reading in the morning and pleasure reading at night.

If you encounter a particularly long article in a magazine and don't have time to read it, tear it out and toss the rest of the magazine. Staple together the pages you've saved, and place it in an On the Go reading file. When you're leaving home and think you might have some spare time, you can grab an article or two or simply take along the whole file. (Be careful that this file doesn't become encyclopedic in size. If it does, all you've accomplished is relocating your problem.)

For other magazines, follow Ronni's rule of Rotation:

- Weekly magazines must be read within a week.

- Monthlies must be read within a month.

- When the new one arrives, toss the old, whether or not it's been read.

Consider subscriptions carefully; no renewal should be automatic. If you find you haven't kept up with a particular title, or if keeping current is causing anxiety, cancel or don't renew.

If you have no specific time for pleasure reading, establish some. Reading just before bed or for thirty minutes early in the evening creates a predictable routine that lets you keep up with material you enjoy. Many find reading time by using odd moments—reading on the exercise bike or by always carrying your own reading material with you so if you have to wait at the dentist or outside a child's dance class, you can use the time for what *you* want. Some families make reading a priority by creating a "reading hour," when everyone sits down and reads to themselves at the same time.

Brochures

Brochures come in the "toss right away" variety and the "possible interest" variety.

Of those that are of possible interest, decide whether or not any action can be taken. If it's a brochure advertising a play that you'd love to attend, check the date and call or send for tickets right away. (If you need to check with another family member, write a note to that effect and leave it in their mail pile.)

Some brochures must be saved until a later date when you'll have a better idea what you want to do. If you know that by March you'll be able to decide about a special weekend-getaway package that was advertised, date-file the brochure in your March tickler file. (For more information, see Chapter 16.) If the brochure describes a quaint inn in Vermont and you have no idea when you might get there, you may want to file the brochure in a Travel file.

Correspondence

Handle as much as you can right away. Correspondence from a company about a bill or a form you need to return to an insurance company should be handled as quickly as possible. If only a signature or some simple piece of information such as your address or Social Security number is required, take care of it right away.

If a letter requires that you investigate old records or something else that is rather time consuming, make a note of it in your master notebook, and file the letter in the appropriate tickler file.

Responding to a personal letter is a leisure time activity, but setting aside time to do it is important if you want to keep up the correspondence. Is this weekend a good time to write back? If not, when would be? Make a reminder note to yourself on your calendar/planner, or your intentions to reply will fall by the wayside. A great time saver: Keep on hand some general "friendship" cards, and mail one off with a few personal lines bringing your correspondent up to date.

SAVE MAIL TIME BY STAYING OFF LISTS

You can save yourself a lot of time (and your mail carrier's back) if you can reduce the mail you receive.

When you shop by mail, order forms often have a question regarding whether or not your name can be sold to other companies. If you want to reduce your mail, check no.

Write to companies asking that they remove your name from their mailing list (create a form letter to save time) and specify that your name should also be removed from any lists they are selling or renting to other companies. Send along the label to facilitate your request. (When writing to catalog companies, write to the address on the label, which is often different from the one from which you would order merchandise.)

When you donate to a charity, enclose a letter saying that you do not want to be on mailing lists that they sell or rent out.

Ask your bank and credit card company to keep you off lists.

When you fill out a new registration form or renew your old one at the Department of Motor Vehicles, read the small print carefully. There is a mail-advertising option you should check off that provides that your name not be made available for mailings.

Write: Mail Preference Service, Direct Marketing Association, P.O. Box 9008, Farmingdale, NY 11735-9008 and ask to be removed from their mailing lists. Provide them with variations of your name: James T, Jim T., J.T., etc. Your name will be put on a mail preference service list that is circulated among national direct mail companies, which will then remove your name from their lists. If you are a regular mail-order customer, this may reduce your mail only slightly, since your name will remain active on lists belonging to companies with whom you do business. The DMA now also runs a telephone preference service that will circulate your name as not interested in telephone solicitations, so contact them while you're at it: Telephone Preference Service, P.O. Box 9014, Farmingdale, NY 11735-9014.

There are several organizations you can join for a small fee that will take additional measures to remove your name from lists. For more information, contact the Stop Junk Mail Association, 800-827-5549, or Private Citizen, 800-CUT-JUNK.

Coping with a Backlog

If you're like most of my clients, today's mail is only a part of the problem. The real paper problem is the mail from the day before and the day before that. One client rarely managed her mail, saying she was too busy with three small children in the household. When her mother-in-law visited twice a year, she routinely handed her baby-sitter a garbage bag, and they would go around the house together scooping mail off surfaces and into the garbage bags, which were then taken to her laundry room. She finally called me for help when her husband was searching for a bank statement, and she had to reveal where she'd been stuffing the old mail!

The good news is that much of your backlog won't be relevant anymore, meaning that you'll be tossing much of what you sort through. The time-consuming news is that you *should* sort through it before tossing it, just in case you've misplaced a check or a few bills.

It's important not to let this task overwhelm you. Think of it as a project you'll whittle away at in small snatches of time. After all, the mail has been aging nicely for however long it's been piled around your house, and it can probably afford to age a little longer. Here's how to do it in four easy steps.

Step One

Go around the house, gathering all the mail that has been collecting in piles, and bring it to one location. For sorting purposes, create one stack of magazines, the other of letters. Unless you're highly energized, that's enough for one day.

Step Two

Plan to spend fifteen to thirty minutes and go through the magazine stack. Toss all catalogs—you're guaranteed to receive a new one soon. As for magazines, virtually all old issues should be "out-placed." (If you haven't read them yet, when *are* you going to? Satisfy your urge to read a magazine with the newest issue and limit it to that.) Donate old copies to a doctor's office, hospital, nursing home, or library or simply place them in your recycling bin.

Step Three

In the next session, plan to spend fifteen minutes sorting through the letters and handling them as you would new mail. Chances are, you will be tossing out a high proportion of this material.

Step Four

Continue working away at your stacks until the job is complete.

Mail Management at the Office

How

Offices generally have a mailbox system or stacking baskets to hold employee mail. The person responsible for sorting office mail should sort it into appropriate piles each day.

The first person to handle your mail—whether it's you or an assistant—should sort through it quickly when it arrives to be certain there is nothing urgent that must be handled immediately. Otherwise, if you go through your own mail, then the process is very similar to handling your mail at home.

Go through it quickly and toss all the mail that is of no relevance to you. Now sort through it more slowly, taking the following actions:

- *Toss* all that you can take care of immediately, whether it involves skimming an announcement or making a note of a meeting date and time.

- *File* all that you need to have on hand. The minutes from the last committee meeting, the documentation of a particular action, a letter that you'll need to refer to later on.

- *Forward* anything that doesn't belong in your office—mail that is incorrectly sent to you or invoices that need your okay and should now go on to Accounting.

■ *Act on* anything that you can. Answer a letter on the bottom of the letter being sent to you, dictate a longer reply, or pick up the telephone and take care of whatever it is that needs to be done. If you delay, the letter will need to be reread and reevaluated, and that wastes extra time.

■ *"To do" later.* Some things simply can't be processed instantly. You may have received an invitation to give a speech. If you plan to do it, there are at minimum three steps involved:

"Today" tasks:

1. Accept the engagement.
2. Note it on your calendar.

For your master notebook:

3. Prepare speech for _____ date.

If You Have an Assistant

Ask your assistant to open everything so that all you need to do is glance through what has arrived. Going through the physical process of opening the mail is a time-consuming job.

An assistant who can take care of the first wave of mail sorting is worth his or her weight in gold. Training someone to do it may require doing it together for several days, but the time investment is worth it.

Establish color-coded file folders in the following categories, and have your assistant sort accordingly:

■ *Urgent*—for anything that requires immediate attention

■ *To Do*—letters to answer; material required to prepare for a meeting, etc.

■ *To Sign*—for letters or anything else requiring a signature such as invoices, purchase orders, staff expenditures, that come through requiring approval

- *To Read*—for magazines, journals, and reports for meetings or special projects

- *To File*—You may want to read some items before they are filed, and this folder lets you check on the To File items before your assistant processes them.

- *To Toss?* If you're not quite certain about the decisions your assistant is making, have him or her place in this file what they intend to throw away. That way you can leaf through it, agreeing or disagreeing with their decisions. After you've had an opportunity to observe your assistant for a few weeks and see that the decisions being made are good ones, you can dispense with this file.

File folders with several items should have a list of the contents (and any relevant deadlines) attached so that you'll know at a glance what you have and what you need to process first.

As your assistant becomes accustomed to the system, teach him or her to pull background information. For example, if you receive a letter referring to previous correspondence, you may want to refer to the original letter, and that should be pulled before giving you the day's mail.

Information in the folders should be passed between the two of you in the correct order. One client constantly pulled items from the folders presented him and mixed them up with other papers. When the assistant received the folders again, her first task was reordering the material so that she could process it appropriately. It took several sessions to convince the boss that he was wasting her time by making her redo a job she had already completed.

What to Do If You Fall Behind

Don't panic! The mail gets ahead of the best of us. If you have a bad week with a work-related or personal crisis, simply take the first opportunity you can to sort through the old mail. Work methodically, tossing as much as you can, and soon you'll be caught up again.

See Chapter 17 for information on e-mail.

Checkpoint and Review

1. Select a clear place to work.

- Have on hand: letter opener, pen, highlighter, adhesive-backed notepads

- Have nearby: wastebasket and/or recycling bin

2. Choose a block of time when you can go through your mail.

Establish a goal of getting through everything before you move on to something else.

3. Home mail:

- Sort by family member.

- Go through your personal stack, handling everything you can at the time:

  - Bills should be filed to be paid approximately two times per month.

  - Dispense with change-of-address cards and appointment reminders immediately.

  - Respond to invitations when they arrive.

  - Toss unwanted solicitations; file those of possible interest with your bills.

  - Toss unwanted catalogs; skim through those of interest or set aside to go through later.

- Put business magazines in your briefcase or near your desk, pleasure magazines on your nightstand or a magazine rack to be read at your leisure. Then find time to do it!

- If a brochure is of interest (telling you of an upcoming theater series), act on it right away. Toss or file all others.

- Answer correspondence as soon as possible; set aside special time to write back to a friend.

4. Save time by having your name removed from mailing lists.

5. Manage your backlog by taking the following steps:

1. Gather all your mail.
2. Spend fifteen to thirty minutes going through all old magazines, tossing as much as you can.
3. Spend your next session going through the letters and handling them as you would new mail.
4. Continue until you're totally caught up.

6. Mail at the office should be sorted into the following categories:

- Toss

- File

- Forward

- Act on

- To Do

7. If you have an assistant:

- Train the assistant to sort your mail into the following categories. Each category should go in a separate file.

- Urgent
- To Do
- To Sign
- To Read
- To File
- To Toss?
- As your assistant becomes accomplished at the job, ask that he or she also pull background material for incoming mail.

CHAPTER 15
· · · · · · · ·

Creating a Filing System That Works

Answer yes or no to the following questions:

	YES	NO
1. Do you have more than one pile of papers on your desk right now?	_____	_____
2. If you have stacks of paper around your office or home, are any of them more than an inch high?	_____	_____
3. The test of a good filing system is retrieval. Could you put your hands on a particular memo within three minutes?	_____	_____

Most people believe in saving papers; few seem to believe in filing them. In my work I have seen the unimaginable: beds, sinks, floors, corners, and closets stuffed with papers, and desks and tables stacked high with teetering piles of files! A very successful businesswoman stuffed everything from invoices to purchase orders under the cushions of her couch. Another couple had two bathrooms and took to using the shower stall of their second bathroom as a repository for clippings.

What most of these people fail to understand is the sole reason for saving a piece of paper is because you think *you might like to look at it again.* "On the dining room table," "under the left cushion," or "by the soap dish" just isn't going to work when it comes to retrieving something important.

In this chapter you'll learn how to establish a filing system that works for you. You'll learn:

- Five easy rules for filing

- The filing "hardware" you'll need and how to use it

- Time-saving tips for filing

Five Easy Rules for Filing

If you're going to get your life under control, you have to set up a good filing system and stick with it, or like any system, it will collapse.

Here are five simple rules to make a filing system work:

1. Have ample space for the amount of paper you need to file. Whether you're filing 15, 150, or 1,500 pieces of paper, you want to have enough space so that papers can be added to files easily, without stuffing.

2. Establish categories that work for you. The headings you create for your files should create an association in your mind that lets you retrieve what you've filed long after you've put it there. For example, if you've just purchased a new computer and want to file away the warranty and other computer-related information, "Computer" is a more logical name than labeling the file according to the make of computer you purchased.

3. File only what you need. Many people save papers, articles, and documents "just in case." Before deciding to file something, ask:

- Do I need to keep it for legal reasons?

- If I really needed to, could I find this information else-where? You may have always dreamed of going to Rome, so you've clipped an article on the wonders of the city. Toss it, because you can find more up-to-date information in a current guidebook if, and when, you actually decide to plan a trip there.

4. Be diligent. File often and file regularly. If you keep up with your filing, it will take only a few minutes.

5. Maintain your files. Create a system for cleaning out your files periodically (once a month, each time you are in a particular file?). Your files will remain more manageable and useful if you remove inactive or unneeded papers regularly.

With these rules in mind, here are some basic guidelines for setting up a filing system that works for you.

The "Hardware"

Purchase a real file cabinet. It's a good investment when you're creating a new filing system. While some people make do with a file-size desk drawer, a small standing file, or a rolling file cart, ultimately you're going to outgrow the space, and purchasing a file cabinet will help you to take the task more seriously.

When selecting a file cabinet, consider the space in your home or office, and select a model that will fit, taking into account the distance needed to open and close the drawers. The most popular styles to choose from are:

A vertical file cabinet. These are standard files with the files running front to back. The drawers generally pull out two feet and provide one row of filing space in each drawer. This style offers the maximum storage in the least amount of space, and the only drawback is that files in the back of the drawer are slightly more difficult to access. Choose from styles that hold legal- or regular-size documents.

A lateral file cabinet. This style of cabinet is wider than it is deep, and the drawers, which generally pull out only a foot, open to reveal files running side to side. This style offers handy desk-side file storage, and a two-drawer system can double as a credenza.

Check that your file cabinets come with a drawer frame. This is necessary for holding suspension files. (Drawer frames can be purchased separately if necessary.)

If you're replacing an existing file system, you can take a measurement of how many "feet" of files you have and use that to judge how many file drawers you'll need for your new system. Plan for three to four inches of unused space in each drawer. That will prevent your files from being "stuffed" from the beginning.

File supplies you'll need include:

Suspension (or hanging) files. The use of suspension files to hold file folders makes a file drawer neater, and gives you easier access to the material within the drawer. These come in various colors so you can include them in any color coding (see below) you choose.

Interior file folders. You're creating a new system, so if your old ones are looking tattered and worn, treat yourself to new supplies and materials. The fresh, neat look to the file drawers may inspire you to keep up with it. Purchase either one-third or one-fifth cut folders for better visibility. And ask for the folder style designed for use in hanging files (they are lower cut). If you intend to color-code, purchase files in a variety of colors.

Plastic tabs and insert labels for the suspension files.

File labels in several colors with coordinating colored pens if ～els are to be handwritten.

Choosing a System That Works for You

For most people a system that combines color coding with alphabetized file names (Anderson to Zipp) or subject groups (all money files together, all health files, etc.) works the best. It's easy to use and to identify the contents.

Color coding offers a strong visual association for retrieval. If blue is the color you've selected for the family medical files, you'll quickly see a blue section within the drawer (hanging file, file folder, and file label can all coordinate). At work, green can represent marketing efforts; yellow can be administrative files; red might represent client folders. This makes it easy for others to keep up the filing system and helps assure that items won't be misfiled. Consider the filing system you're establishing, and then determine what will work best for you.

Selecting file names is the next important step. What you file will depend on how you select the names. Subject files (entertaining, summer camp options, travel, etc.) may serve your needs, or you may prefer name filing (Jones Account, Smith Account, etc.). When you select the names under which you'll file, be certain that the name is one that will remain meaningful to you. Ask yourself: "When and how will I want to retrieve this?"

The best name for a travel folder is Travel or the destination, England, rather than using a title that is unclear or unspecific (such as the name of your travel agency). Or if you have a file of catalogs from which you want to order by mail, group them under Mail-Order Catalogs rather than filing each by name.

Ten Time-Saving Filing Tips

- When you receive a piece of paper to be filed, date it, note the source, and write the name of the file where it's to be placed. You'll avoid having to reread it to check on its contents or what you intended to do with it. And if there is a time when the information will become obsolete, write "Destroy after _____" on the document.

- Papers that belong together should be stapled, not clipped. Paper clips catch on other papers and lead to missing papers within a file. Special clip links can bolt hanging files together to prevent papers from slipping between the files.

- Don't ever pile. If you're starting a new project, create a file for it the first day it arrives on your desk.

- Organize within the file. The subject may break down into logical subject groupings: your family file might be divided up by family member, or by related information, all medical reports together, or all test scores, etc. If timing is important, an easy way to do this is by simply placing new papers at the front of the file. That way you've created a file that is sequential as to date.

- Certain files may be more helpful if they are alphabetical. When filing by name, put last name first.

- If more than one person uses this filing system, create a master directory listing all the subjects within. Keep this list at the front of the first filing drawer for easy reference.

- Have an "out" card system. If you remove a file or a paper from a file for any period of time, leave a note as to the whereabouts of the item so that you'll be reminded why something isn't there.

- File regularly. People have different preferences. Some do it at the end of each day (which is most efficient for organizing your desk and your time and for being prepared for the next day's activities); others like to do it weekly, but all people who have a useful filing system have one thing in common: *they file regularly.*

- Weed out frequently. Whenever you have a file out, sort through it (a great activity to do when you're left on hold on the telephone) and toss what you don't need. On the inside of the folder note the date on which you last sifted through it; that way you'll know at a glance if you haven't been through the file in a very long time.

- Within your filing system, create an area for inactive files. Select one of the least accessible drawers for this designation. Every six months, cull through your current files and transfer those you haven't used recently to the inactive status. This keeps the files easily accessible to you until you're positive the file is indeed inactive, but it frees up space in your current drawers so that filing and retrieval is still performed easily. When you go through your files again in six months, those in the inactive area that are still untouched should be sorted again. Toss or recycle what you can and put the rest in a cardboard file box for basement or closet storage.

HOW TO FIND A MISSING PAPER

- Recheck the file folder where it should be. Perhaps it's caught within the file.

- Now check the folders in front and in back of where this folder was. Perhaps the paper was simply misfiled.

- Was the information confusing, and therefore would someone have filed it under something else?

- Who else might have taken the file? Ask them if they have it.

Conduct a Filing "Check-Up"

If you're finding it difficult to locate much of what you've filed, use this system to conduct a check-up.

- Are you up to date with your filing? You'd be surprised how many missing papers are found in to-file bins and drawers.

- Are your labels or files worn out and catching on other things?

- Are you using too many folders? Many thin files are as complicated to look through as many single pieces of paper.

- Are your files too stuffed? If a folder gets too thick, the papers creep up and block the heading. If this is happening with any of your files, go through the file. Can you recycle or toss some of the papers, or should you create a new folder for the overflow?

- Are your drawers overloaded? When you access a file within a drawer, you ought to have enough space to have a "working V" as you look down into the file. If you don't have extra space in each drawer, you need to weed out.

Tickler (or Reminder) Files

The tickler-file system is a great time saver that reminds you of what you need to know when you need to know it, without bogging you down ahead of time.

Tickler files are your "action" files; your future to-do list with backup copy (tickets you need for an upcoming trip, a memo for an office meeting on Monday). The system provides a logical way to locate needed items as well as remind yourself of things you must do or calls you must make on a specific date in the future. Here's how to create one:

- Select thirteen file folders and labels. To color-code, select a specific color for this group of files.

- Label a folder for each month with one labeled "This Week."

   (Clients in office settings often like a tickler file for each day, so in addition to the set of twelve for the month, take ~irty-one additional folders and mark one for each date.)

These folders are where you'll put papers that require action but you don't intend to take care of today. Some examples include the following:

- A flier describing your child's class trip in two days, complete with directions as to exactly how their lunches must be bagged, should go in your This Week file (or, using the expanded tickler file system, in a file for a special date).

- Directions to an event you're attending next month belong in the folder for the appropriate month.

- A letter you've written that you'll need to follow up on if you haven't heard within a month should go in next month's file.

- A perfect birthday card for someone whose birthday is July 15 (and it's only April now) should go in the July file.

- A reminder to make an appointment for your annual physical, a mammogram, an eye exam, your six-month dental visits—each occurring at different times of the year.

It's the perfect way to manage those papers that are temporarily vital to your life.

Checkpoint and Review

1. Follow these five easy rules for filing:

- Have ample room for the files you need.

- Create logical categories for your files.

- Limit what you file to items you really need.

- Be diligent.

- Maintain your files regularly.

2. Select a good file cabinet, and purchase the accessories

(suspension files, file folders, and labels) you need to establish a useful and convenient system.

3. Decide on a filing method that works for you.

- Color-code if you can.

- Create file names that are as logical for the subject today as they will be in six months.

4. Conduct periodic file check-ups.

- Are you caught up on all your filing?

- Are your files too stuffed?

- Are your drawers too loaded?

- Take care of what you need to so that your system will continue to support your quests to find what you need.

5. Use tickler files to hold your to-do items of the future.

CHAPTER 16

· · · · · · · ·

Computers, the Internet, and Faxes:
The Information Explosion

The time-saving possibilities offered by the computer (and all its capabilities, including online and Internet access), home fax machines, and other technological advances have changed our lives. There are so many advantages!

Just think of the special conveniences possible on a home computer:

- Organize your time with special planner programs (see Chapter 4) and create a telephone directory that works for you.

- Utilize any one of the specialty programs—from graphic design and mailing lists to travel planners and recipe files—to make your life more convenient.

- Use the computer to manage personal and business finances.

- Use word processing to make writing and rewriting much faster and easier.

Those are just the benefits on a home PC. Think about how much better and easier computers have made work life in offices, manufacturing plants, and stores of all types!

Next, consider your basic home computer with a modem added. What do you have? Access to innumerable resources via online services and the Internet.

These technological advances are so mind-boggling they make the "lowly" fax machine look primitive, but in essence this ability to send printed words through telephone wires is nothing short of amazing. Regular mail, messengers, and overnight mail move slowly when compared to the rapid-fire transmission of faxes.

Amazing as it all is, be forewarned. For technology to be a strong time-management tool, it must be managed. Listen to what happened to these people as they were moving ahead in the world of technology:

"My boss is constantly faxing me things on the weekend. I try to preserve Saturday and Sunday as family time, but it's hard when stuff from work is always coming in," reports a young mother.

"I designed a flier on the computer last night, and it looks great, but it took me forever to do," says a client whose specialty is *writing* the copy for fliers.

"I didn't get to bed last night until one a.m.," says another fellow. "I dropped into an online chat room, and it was really interesting. I just couldn't quit."

"I get so much e-mail! If I answered it all, I wouldn't have time to do anything else," laughs a friend.

Just because you receive a fax at 10:09 A.M., you don't have to answer it at 10:10. And yes, you can volunteer to write a flier for the school on your PC, but must you also be responsible for designing the graphics? And as for online services and the World Wide Web—wonderful resources, but oh, so time-consuming! You have to set limits.

Technology is changing so quickly that it's hard to be fully current. The best advice I can give you is to stay tuned for new developments. In the meantime, this chapter offers some basic guidelines on some of the time-saving technologies you can benefit from and how to manage them. We'll examine:

- The computer
- Online services and the Internet
- E-mail
- Fax machines

The Computer

If you've not yet invested in a computer or are thinking about upgrading, remember:

Select the most recent model and ask the salesperson about how easy it will be to upgrade (technology is changing so rapidly that you want your computer to be as current as possible).

Opt for one with a large memory. Many of the software programs take up a great deal of space on the hard drive, and you'll want your computer drive to be big enough to handle the programs that interest you.

Be sure the computer you select has a warranty. If there's going to be a problem, it generally happens soon after purchase.

You should also check out a CD-ROM. Once you've seen an encyclopedia on CD-ROM, it will be very difficult to go back to thumbing through a hardbound-book edition. The same goes for many of the games, programs, and books that have been put on CD—they're amazing!

Watch prices on scanners. These scan pictures and text and bring them into your computer. By using a scanner, you can see a family photograph on screen, or work on a letter that you never had to keyboard into your machine. At some point these will be an integral part of home computers. Currently manufacturers are making it easy to touch up and store family photographs on computer. As the technology improves and the prices drop, the uses will grow.

Take safety precautions. Invest in an anti-virus program. The odds of getting a virus on a home machine are low, but if it should happen, it can wipe out years of work in seconds. The best way to prevent a virus is to try to avoid them (like staying away from people with colds when you want to stay healthy). Avoid swapping floppy disks and program files with other computers; this includes being wary of the free disks that come in the mail for you to "test." In addition, invest in an anti-virus program. All major online services and bulletin boards allow you to download them, and you can get updates. Look for a virus-protection utility that scans boot records, data files, and programs in search of lurking viruses. If you rarely install new software or use other people's floppy disks, run a virus scan once every few months. If you install new software or swap floppies frequently, it's wise to run a scan once a week.

Maximizing Use of Your Computer

Everyone needs a computer "wizard" (someone who will diagnose why the latest program you purchased isn't working properly and get it going for you), so locate an expert—then you'll have his or her telephone number when you need it. Ask at local computer stores, check the yellow pages, or call anywhere that teaches computer basics. (Don't be surprised when your wizard arrives in an eighteen-year-old body; some of the best are students.) Later on, if you have the time to gain this expertise yourself, it can be invaluable, or better yet, see if you can't "grow" your own computer wizard by encouraging one of your kids to gain this expertise. Having at least one expert in the family is ideal.

Your hard disk will operate more efficiently if you organize it. Ask about an optimization program that can clean up your disk so that the data is stored as efficiently as possible.

If you don't already know how to organize within your system, hire your computer wizard to come and get you started. IBM compatibles have a logical directory and subdirectory system while Macintosh users work with folders. A good way to manage projects is to establish a general directory (folder for Mac users) for a topic, and within that directory you can create subdirectories or files. Think of your system as containing trees with branches. You might have one tree (directory) you label for your daughter, "Mary," and everything Mary works on will be her branches (subdirectories). Your home computer might have a "Work" directory and a directory for items pertaining to a specific volunteer organization. Within those categories you could have the work divided into subdirectories and files.

Make your file names meaningful. A good name will tell you the project, the type of file and what version it is. School3.ltr, might refer to the third version of a letter you were preparing for a school. Computer file names should be consistent with names used for paper files to avoid confusion.

One of the benefits of having a computer is not having to create from scratch. Create form letters for any type of correspondence you send out regularly, and make a template for recurring reports (expense reports, etc.) so that you can copy the basics and insert the new data each month.

Clean out your files regularly. Delete duplicates and files you won't use again. Transfer inactive files you don't need right away to a floppy disk. Your computer will be faster once the data is pared down.

If you have information you've copied to floppy disks, be sure to label them all (keep a paper printout of the floppy's directory so that you'll have a quick reference sheet telling exactly what is on each disk). If any of it is data that you are keeping for a prolonged period, recopy it annually, since disks fade over time. Store in a storage case protected from heat, light, dust, and magnetization.

To keep your computer machinery clean on the outside, use a compressed-air spray (available at computer and photo-supply stores) to blow dust from between your keys. A mini-vacuum (especially for computers) also comes in handy. To clean the monitor, use a cloth lightly moistened with glass cleaner (don't spray anything directly onto the monitor).

Long after your warranty expires, keep learning about your computer. Most people learn only what they need to know, and as a result they use only a fraction of their machine's capabilities:

- Fill out the postcard that comes with any computer program you buy, and the company will make you aware of updates.

- For more general information, pick up a computer magazine (look for one for the layperson) now and then and see what's new.

- Expand your knowledge regularly by making an appointment on your calendar to teach yourself (or get someone to teach you) something new. The more you learn, the more time you'll save.

KEEPING YOUR DATA KID-SAFE

To avoid having your six-year-old enter a few additional numbers to your family finance program or switch around some of the sentences in one of your letters, create an "adult" section in your computer as well as one for your kids:

- Supervise younger children when they are on the computer, and teach older ones which areas are yours alone.

- Use the password-protection option found on many screen savers to keep kids out of areas they shouldn't be in. Many of the new home PC systems come preloaded with a program navigator that allows you to password-protect programs and files on your hard disk.

Guarding Against the Unthinkable

For any regular computer user, the single biggest time waster is having your computer crash—figuring out what you lost, deciding if it can be retrieved, working to re-install the data that is missing—it takes a lot of time and a lot of worry.

You have to protect yourself. Experts say that it isn't *whether* your computer will crash, it's *when*. Since computers can and do freeze up and get viruses, you must copy your data regularly to avoid losing it:

Invest in a tape backup system if you use your computer regularly. These systems are simple, easy to use, reliable, and fast. When purchasing a system, be certain that the one you're buying is adequate for backing up what your computer holds.

Once you have your backup system installed, you'll need to make a habit of copying your computer drive (or selected files) regularly, so establish a set schedule for backing up. If a home computer is primarily used for games and school work, then backing up once a month will keep you current. Set a date, perhaps the first of each month, and write it in your daily planner.

If you use your computer frequently, back up at least weekly or whenever you've entered a lot of information. (This is vital if you're keeping financial records on it.)

At work (or if you're using the computer intensively at home), your backup should be on three levels—a monthly, weekly, and daily backup:

- Once a month make a complete backup of your hard drive using the tape backup system. This should be saved until it is replaced the following month. If your computer picks up a virus sometime during the month, you'll have this clean copy to help in reconstructing what was on your machine.

- A full backup should be done weekly and saved from week to week.

- Every night, evaluate what you have done on the computer. You may not need to create a full backup, but you should use a disk to copy any files in which you've made significant changes. If you decide not to back up on any given evening, be certain to print out what you were working on. If the worst should happen, you at least have a paper copy and could scan it in or retype it.

Your monthly backup copy should be kept off premises. Consider taking your work backup copy with you when you go home, and take your home copy to work. If you're working on something particularly important, drop your daily backup in your briefcase every night.

Many companies actually run two backup copies of important data to protect against something happening to one copy. There will be times when this is a wise precaution.

ABOUT BACKING UP

Total Backup. This saves everything on your hard drive.
Selective Backup. When you back up selectively, you choose to have copied specific directories and files.
Modified Backup. This provides for backing up only the files that have been changed since your last backup.

IS THE WWW FOR YOU, AND WHAT IS IT ANYWAY?

The World Wide Web is the most usable feature of the Internet, a worldwide network of computers. The Internet includes access to huge machines at universities and corporations that store vast volumes of publicly available material, including text, pictures, sound, and video that you may find useful or interesting for business, education, or entertainment.

To tap into the "web," you need a commercial access provider like one of the major online services or a smaller firm that advertises web access. You'll also need one or more software programs that will let you dial into the access provider and browse the web.

The World Beyond—Electronically Speaking

No doubt about it, the world is going online and cruising the information highway. If you want to know more about an illness, need information on a foreign country you plan to visit, or are conducting technical research for a project, you have access to everything from scholarly journals and consumer magazines to real people who will offer comments and advice when asked. The time it takes? After you turn on your computer, you can have this information delivered into your machine within minutes, and you haven't even left home!

- Invest in a high-speed modem. Technology constantly improves, and you'll want to start with the best that's available.

- If you're adding a modem to an older machine, call your computer wizard to set up your system. You'll save time by using an expert.

- Consider running a dedicated phone line for your modem (perhaps combine it with a fax line). One phone line for all telephone/fax/modem needs in a "wired" home will no longer be enough.

- Talk to others about which online service is for you. You may find that in your profession, the forums are more active in one service than another, or you may decide that a local service that provides access to the Internet is what suits your needs best.

- If you're using an online service, it becomes expensive to stay online. Purchase an *offline reader/navigator* program that lets you capture your mail, news, and messages from your favorite forum more efficiently. It can decrease your online time considerably by letting you download and respond to e-mail and forum messages offline.

- You need only pick up a daily newspaper to realize that some of what is on the Internet is not appropriate for children. Most of the online services have reworked their systems so that parents can limit their children's access to certain areas of the service and the Internet. If you have children in the household, investigate what protection services are currently being offered and consider which is best for your family.

E-Mail

Once you have a modem and are connected through an online or e-mail service, you can receive electronic mail, a very efficient form of communication—no stamp, envelope, or paper, just a paragraph or two sent directly (and almost instantly) to the person you intend. It's a quick way to exchange personal messages or important documents when you can't get together in person.

People are finding that it's a great way to communicate within branch offices or for telecommuters to stay in touch, but it also works for family members or friends (particularly those in different time zones). Your college-age kids may rarely write you a real letter, but if you set up to communicate with them via e-mail, chances are you'll hear almost daily. (With e-mail it takes only a minute or two to respond.)

Sign up with an online service, e-mail service, or one of the new consumer-oriented services that offer access to the Internet. To use e-mail effectively:

- Keep e-mail addresses in your online address book for easy sending, but note them in your regular address book so that you can stay in touch even when you're out of town and without your home PC.

- Write after hours—it's cheaper because rates are lower, and it's faster because of less cyber traffic.

- Use the subject line (the space where you announce the reason for writing) to stress importance. Tell the major reason for your communication or use it to catch attention.

- Try to keep your message to one screen. If you need to send something long, attach it as a separate document.

- Phrase your message so that what you need is clear, and make it easy for them to reply.

- Use "urgent message" notations sparingly.

- Don't write controversial messages in e-mail. Those types of messages are better if handled by phone or by letter.

If you're overwhelmed by your e-mail:

- Set aside a specific time every day to go through your e-mail, and read and answer it in order of priority. When you run out of time, scan the list and decide who, if anyone, still needs a reply. If they do, take care of it. If not, read the messages and delete all that you received for that day.

- Check your e-mail box regularly, but don't let the arrival of e-mail interrupt you. Turn off any device on your computer that beeps when e-mail arrives. It should be handled at your convenience, not just because it's there.

- Don't fill out forms that ask for personal information, unless you want people to contact you regarding certain subjects.

- Check out special mail-preference services that allow you to stop unsolicited mail.

- Ask to be taken off mailing lists or if you're copied on letters to other people at work, ask to be removed from their cc: list.

WHEN A COMPUTER WASTES YOUR TIME

Despite the time-saving gift of the computer, there are times when it wastes time:

1. Games. Like anything else you do for pleasure, you need to consider how and when you play your computer games. If you enjoy relaxing with a computer game for fifteen to thirty minutes in the evening, then that's a great way to unwind. If you find yourself clicking to a game instead of your work, then your computer becomes a time trap.

2. The online chat rooms and exploring the online services. This can be addictive and expensive! If you use it the way you would sit down and have a cup of coffee with a friend, that's fine. If the online or Internet access begins to take over your life, you'll need to exert more control.

3. The voluminous material now available through your home computer. Think of it. A third-grade student can access enough information on dinosaurs to write a major thesis. Whether it's you or your child who is being overwhelmed by voluminous amounts of research after the flick of a few keys, keep it in perspective. Just because you can print out a hundred pages on any given topic doesn't mean you have to use—or even read—all of it.

4. Taking on too much. Now with a computer you can write an ad for a volunteer organization, and they can ask you to design it as well. The only problem is that if you don't do that every day, it can be very time-consuming. Set limits on how you are willing to use your computer time. Maybe you can still write the ad to help out, but one of their other members with expertise can handle the design end.

Have Computer, Will Travel

If you travel, you'll want to equip yourself so that you don't have to leave your computer behind. In addition to a laptop computer, you'll want to:

- Ask about the cables that permit you to download from your regular computer to your laptop without having to do the transfer by copying onto floppies.

- Invest in a computer travel kit and keep it permanently packed. You'll want a modem card, a modular jack (for connecting your modem in a hotel room), an adapter (for foreign travel), and appropriate local area access numbers as well as telephone numbers for technical support.

- Book a hotel room with modem data port accessibility.

The Home Fax Machine

When you've called for information and someone says, "I could send it to you right away if you have a fax machine," wouldn't it be nice to say, "Go ahead"?

Home fax machines offer many benefits—you can stay in touch with the office if you need to, be in instant communication with distant family members if both houses are equipped, receive information you call for instantly, and mail-order by fax. What's more, a fax machine can double as a copy machine for making a few photocopies. There's no doubt it saves time.

When purchasing a fax machine, you'll be selecting either a machine that uses thermal paper or a plain paper fax machine. The machine model using thermal paper—a slick paper that comes on rolls and tends to curl—is less expensive and is perfectly usable for families when the faxes will be read and tossed. If you run a home business or if you will need to preserve your faxes for any reason, you're better off spending more money on a plain paper model.

Within each model are various levels of features. Some have speed dialing, most have memory (so that an incoming fax can be stored if you are low on ink or out of paper), and most have a broadcast feature that permits you to send one fax to several different numbers. Fax manufacturers are currently adding features to make them more desirable for personal use. Right now models are being created that also serve as answering machines. Keep looking for what you want.

Fax machines are often put on your regular telephone line. However, home business owners or those who have call waiting (fax machines and call waiting are not compatible) will want to investigate having a dedicated line.

Like junk mail, there are junk faxes. Government regulators are examining this, but currently your best solution is to fax back to the offending machine requesting that your number be removed from the list.

There's a tendency to assume that anything sent by fax requires an instant reply. That isn't true. When you get the fax, *you* decide when you're ready to fax back.

Checkpoint and Review

1. When shopping for a computer or considering an upgrade:

- Get the most recent model, and purchase one with a large memory.

- Add a CD-ROM and a scanner when you can.

- Invest in an anti-virus program.

2. To get the best use out of your computer, take the following steps:

- Find a wizard who will help you when you need it.

- Use an optimization program to organize your hard drive.

- Set up a logical filing system with meaningful names.

- Clean your files regularly.

- Keep current on computers and make it a priority to keep learning about your computer.

- Use systems that restrict your children's access to your financial and word-processing files.

- *Back up your data.*

3. To enjoy the Web and online services:

- Invest in a high-speed modem if your computer does not already have one.

- Consider adding a dedicated telephone line.

- Investigate various services. If you have kids, ask about what provisions are made for limiting access for children.

- Get an offline navigator so that you can save money by working offline.

4. E-mail is a wonderful tool, but like anything else, it must be managed.

- Respond at your convenience.

- Keep your messages short.

- Be specific about the action you hope will be taken.

5. Don't let the computer waste your time.

- Set limits on game and online usage.

- Don't feel compelled to read, answer, or do everything just because it's there.

6. Use your home fax machine as an additional time saver for faxing and small copy jobs.

- Select a model (choose from plain or thermal paper) with add-ons that appeal to you.

- Don't feel compelled to answer instantly just because a fax has arrived.

Section 5

TIME TRAPS

CHAPTER 17

. . . .

Interruptions

Interruptions are the number one obstacle we face when it comes to controlling our time.

Does this home scene sound familiar? It's late afternoon, and you've just come in from the freezing cold after doing a long list of errands. You settle the kids with a snack and a twenty-five-minute videotape, and you fix yourself a nice cup of hot tea and finally sit down to glance through the morning newspaper. Then:

- The doorbell rings—package delivery.

- The dog is banging at the back door, telling you it's way too cold outside and that he's missed you.

- The kids finished their snack, and they've sent a "representative" to the kitchen to ask for more.

- The phone rings; it's your mother-in-law. Much as you love her, you didn't really want to speak to her right now.

You're left thinking, "Was one simple cup of tea and a twenty-minute break too much to ask? In a delightful children's story,

Five Minutes Peace by Jill Murphy, Mrs. Large, an elephant, learns about how impossible it is to find uninterrupted peace. When she sneaks away for a quiet bath, one son comes to play her a tune on his flute, her daughter invites herself in to read her "Little Red Riding Hood," and the baby brings bath toys for Mrs. Large to enjoy. Before you know it, they're all in the tub together. In the end she moves to the kitchen, where she has three minutes and forty-five seconds to read the newspaper before they all come to be with her.

Even if you are single or your kids are long gone, your life still holds plenty of potential for interruption, both during times when you'd like a break and times when you've planned to focus on a task that requires concentration. The phone rings at the most inconvenient times, and it always seems as though drop-in visitors show up when you're least expecting them.

At the office it only gets worse. The calls never stop, the fax machine spews paper at will, and in all likelihood you have lots of people around you, meaning that an ever increasing group may come trooping to your desk to ask for something, tell you something, or simply stop to visit.

Whether you're at home or work, unremitting interruptions are stressful. You're there with something you need to get done or are taking a well-deserved break, and you're faced with so many interruptions that it begins to look more likely that you'll climb Mount Everest than finish what you're doing.

What to do? Stand up for yourself. If you don't step in and begin to control as many interruptions as you can, you'll never be able to have the focused time you need and deserve.

Interruption management is best handled with a two-step plan:

1. Anticipate interruptions so you can reduce or manage them.
2. Shorten those that occur.

We'll also look at ways to

- Maintain your focus despite interruptions.

- Identify your worst interrupters.

- Conquer the self-interrupting habit.

- Cope with an "interrupted kind of day."

Anticipate Interruptions in Order to Reduce or Manage Them

Many interruptions that occur are ones you could have foreseen. If you and your children have just returned home from a long day of school and work, you're almost guaranteed numerous interruptions about homework and plans for the next day. At work, if a new employee has been on the job for only three or four days, you can imagine that members of the department will have to interrupt their own work to help out now and then. Here's what you can do to anticipate and thereby reduce or manage some interruptions:

Be realistic about how much time you can preserve as uninterrupted time. Most people can probably protect only about an hour, though some may be lucky enough to set aside as many as three hours. If you accept that you have to be open to interruptions at some point, it may be easier to protect the small amount of time you're trying to claim as your own.

Group interruptions that you know about. At work, schedule all your appointments during a block of time in the morning or afternoon. At home, try to arrange that the sofa you've ordered will be delivered on the same day that the dishwasher repairman has agreed to come.

Some telephone calls can be channeled into more convenient times by letting regular callers know when it's best to reach you. At home, it may be convenient to make and receive phone calls from 7:30 to 8:30 P.M. When you speak to people, be it an aunt who lives across the country or your friend who checks in regularly, let them know that you're usually home then and that it's a good time for you to talk. (It's certainly a popular time for telemarketers to call, so you might as well take calls from people you like then, too!) At work you may designate afternoons as a time when you're in and available for whatever comes your way. If you let people know it's a good time to reach you, chances are they'll be delighted.

Make family members and co-workers as independent of you as possible. Consider:

- What is the most frequent reason someone interrupts you?

- Is there a way to arrange for them to take care of the matter themselves?

In anticipation of youngsters who may need a snack, try providing a child-size pitcher on a low shelf of the refrigerator to enable children four and up to pour milk or juice for themselves. Keep available cut-up fruit, peeled carrot sticks and crackers just for the taking. Cups, bowls, and napkins can also be left where they are accessible to junior members of the family.

If co-workers come to you seeking information, is there a way they could find those answers themselves? Or could they e-mail you and you'll answer when you go through the rest of your mail? Or can the matter simply wait until you've finished the task at hand? If you are the employer or manager of a group of people, prepare a "what to know and where to find it" handbook answering the most commonly asked questions for a new employee.

Establish systems that prevent the need for interruptions. If you have a co-worker or an assistant with whom you work closely, establish a daily meeting time so that you can discuss the known items that you're both working on during the day. While there may still be some unexpected issues that come up, you will have reduced the number by covering much of the information at a scheduled meeting.

Trade "coverage" with your spouse or a co-worker: "I'll take care of things for the next hour if you'll take over for an hour later on."

Seem less available so that you're not anyone's first choice. At the office, angle your desk so that people don't catch your eye as they walk past; at home, don't expect to find peace in the kitchen. Remove yourself from the household traffic pattern and settle in for some quiet time in a more remote area of the house.

Anticipate the results of new occurrences. If it's raining when you awaken one morning, get out your family's rain gear while you're getting out your own so that you needn't stop and do it later. At work, if you're the right-hand person to someone who has been away, clear your schedule so that you'll have time available to help him catch up.

Establish "interruption-free" time and do what you can to protect it.

- At home and at work, screen calls through voice mail or an answering machine.

- Close the door. At home you may need a "Do Not Disturb" sign so that family members get the message.

- One home-based entrepreneur says: "We have a rule in our family that the kids are not to interrupt me during a business phone call unless they are bleeding or it's life and death."

- If you work in an open office without doors, go to an empty conference room or office for your interruption-free time or leave the premises. Some people go to the library or a coffee shop and get work done there.

Shorten Those That Occur

There will always be interruptions that you cannot prevent. What you can do is manage them. Here are some strategies.

Learn to keep your own priorities on top. Try saying: "Could we talk about that in a few minutes? I have something here I need to finish." Or ask: "How much time do you need?" If the interrupter needs more than five minutes, ask that the two of you agree on a different time to meet.

Learn to say, "Not now." Often the interrupter hasn't even noticed that you're busy (or simply taking a well-deserved break). Say that you'll help them, and then estimate the time when you'll be available. To six-year-old Sam who wants to dig in the garden: "I'll meet you outside in fifteen minutes." And to Mary at the office who needs some information about your travel schedule: "I'll give you those dates in about thirty minutes, when I'm finished here."

Often the interrupter could be helped rather quickly if they would just get to the point. Try saying: "How can I help you?" It helps direct their thoughts and establishes that this is not a time for chatting.

If your boss is a frequent interrupter, dropping off more "urgent" work for you to do, you'll need to have priority discussions now and then. "I've been working on a plan for our sales conference and I know it's important, but with all the other things that have come up, I just haven't been able to finish what I need to. Could we talk about what I have left to do and what you need to have me finish first?" Like everyone else, bosses frequently focus on clearing *their* desks, not worrying about yours. Once the situation is brought to his or her attention, you may be pleasantly surprised by how reasonable your supervisor can be. When you are interrupted, make the following evaluations:

- Am I the only one who can help this person?

- How much time will this take?

- If I let them interrupt me, what am I losing?

Don't prolong an interruption. Once you know what is needed and have evaluated what you're going to do about it, go back to what you were doing. Often people succumb to the interruption and encourage the interrupter to stay. The next thing you know you're in the midst of a twenty-minute conversation about their trip to the Rockies.

Consider what you can do once you are interrupted. You can file while chatting with a co-worker who has just returned from a trip. You can do a host of household tasks while the repairman is there, and a long cord on a kitchen telephone will permit you to unload the dishwasher or prepare a full meal while talking on the phone.

Involve the interrupter. A co-worker who ends up helping you collate a report may think twice before dropping in unexpectedly, while a child or spouse may actually be quite happy to be included in your project with a task geared to their level and interest.

Stand up. If someone has dropped into your office "just for a minute," continuing the conversation while standing prevents them from relaxing and gives them the cue that it's time to leave. If that doesn't work, ask if they'd like to walk somewhere with you. That limits the amount of your time they can take because you are now in control of what time you walk back.

If there's a well-known time waster at your office, set up a system with colleagues. Ask that they phone you with an "emergency" five minutes or so after your talkative co-worker has descended upon you.

Maintaining Focus Despite Interruptions

If interruptions are bound to happen, the next challenge is keeping each one in its place—as a small break in your work, not a major disruption. Here's what to do:

If you're doing desk work or serious thinking when interrupted, make a note of what your current thoughts were. If your work involves reading or reviewing material, mark where you left off.

If you get in the habit of writing down steps of a project (see Chapter 8), it will permit you to leave something and come back more easily. If you've listed seven tasks in an overall project, and you're interrupted after task 2, check off the first two tasks so that when you return you're ready to start with task 3.

If the interruption is something that must be taken care of, evaluate whether your response could be delayed for a bit while you finish what you're working on. If you're going to have to focus on the new priority now, then take a look at your calendar to schedule time to work on the project you have to abandon temporarily.

If you've been interrupted several times, it's very tempting to simply give up and quit. Unless you foresee that the day has simply gone out of control, try not to get discouraged. Go back and complete your goal for that day.

Conducting an Interruption Check-up

If you're still puzzled about why your time is so fractured, conduct an "interruption check-up." This involves keeping an "Interruption Log" for a week. Make one similar to this:

WHO	WHEN	WHAT	HOW LONG

After tracking your interruptions for a week, begin to look for patterns:

- Are the same people responsible for the majority of your interruptions? Once you recognize who is creating most of your interruptions, there are generally steps you can take to make them less dependent on you during specific blocks of time.

- Could their interruption have been anticipated? If you've anticipated their needs, you ought to be able to prevent the interruption.

- Could it have waited? Next time you'll remember to say, "Not now, but later."

- If the disruption turns out to be a group who has gathered outside your door to chat, try closing your door, and if that isn't possible, ask them nicely if they couldn't move their conversation elsewhere for today. Over time they will develop a new place to hang out.

Conquering the Self-Interrupting Habit

What is self-interrupting? It's when, in the process of trying to do one thing, we decide to focus on something else. Take this quiz to learn whether you have the habit of interrupting yourself:

	FREQUENTLY	SOMETIMES	NEVER
1. When you're working on a project, does your mind drift to other things?	____	____	____
2. While working, if you think of an important phone call, do you stop to make it?	____	____	____
3. Do you take breaks while working on a project even though you're not at a very good stopping place?	____	____	____
4. Do you find that once you've started something you often have to jump up and down, getting supplies or equipment you need?	____	____	____
5. Do you sometimes find that the time you've set aside is gone, but you haven't accomplished what you intended?	____	____	____

If most of your answers fell into the "frequently" or "sometimes" category, then you can gain extra time by learning not to interrupt yourself. Here's what you should know:

Self-interrupting generally becomes worse at two distinct times:

1. When you don't want to do something, it serves as an excellent form of procrastination.
2. When you've been interrupted so much by forces beyond your control, your ability to focus is weaker and so you find that you're constantly interrupting yourself.

Here's what you can do to break this habit:

Make your environment more conducive to concentration:

- If you're trying to get desk work done, then make certain your desk surface is clear (see Chapter 22). If you remove temptation (other things to do) from your sight (regardless of what your project is or where you're doing it), you'll find it easier to work.

- Before you start work, make certain you have the supplies or equipment you need. If you're packing up a box to be mailed and your labels are in one room and your tape in another (offering an excellent opportunity for self-interrupting), the job will take extra time because you haven't collected what you need.

Once you've established time to work on something, make a pact with yourself to focus on the task at hand. If you've been in the habit of interrupting yourself a great deal, set small goals: "I'll work on this for fifteen minutes, and then I'll take a break (or make a phone call or whatever you'd rather be doing)." By building up to longer work periods gradually, you'll strengthen your power of concentration and your desire to have this focused time for what you need to do. Don't start another project without finishing the one you're working on.

Concentration radiates its own protective shield. Co-workers or family members may walk in and realize that you're really busy. Don't look up, and resist the urge to begin a conversation by asking what they want. They're exhibiting good sense by leaving you alone, so let them.

Even when you've been interrupted, try to get back to your work and meet whatever goal it is that you've set for the day.

Don't procrastinate! (See Chapter 18.)

An Interrupted Kind of Day

Not very long ago a client was describing to me a day that had gone out of control. She'd been at work only to receive a phone call from the school telling her that one of her children was sick and needed to go home. She left her office with her current work incomplete, picked up her child, and made a stop at the pediatrician's for a throat culture. Then they went home. "I should have been delighted to have some extra time at home. John settled in to watch television, but I just couldn't focus on anything. There were a few phone calls and then John needed a snack, and before I knew it, it was time to pick up the other kids at school. Every time I would try to think about doing something—even going through the mail or starting a laundry—I just couldn't focus on getting anything done."

On days when our plans begin to unravel, we're often like a helicopter having difficulty finding a place to land. We cruise and we hover, but nothing feels right, so we get nothing done. The solution? Get involved in completing just one thing— maybe something as simple as opening the mail. As soon as you experience the satisfaction of committing to one task, you'll find it easier to settle down and do something else without constantly interrupting yourself and quitting before you've even begun.

Checkpoint and Review

1. Anticipate interruptions in order to manage or reduce them.

- Group expected interruptions like appointments or necessary phone conversations.

- Encourage independence of family members and co-workers.

- Establish systems (such as a regular daily meeting with an assistant or co-worker) to prevent the need for interruptions.

- Remove yourself physically from the main flow of traffic so that you're not interrupted unnecessarily.

2. When an interruption occurs, do what you can to make it brief.

- Learn to say, "Not now."

- Indicate that the interrupter should get right to the point.

- If the problem sounds time-consuming, see if you can get back to them later.

- Be certain you're the person they really need.

- Don't prolong the interruption.

- Use body language to indicate that their time is up.

3. When you are interrupted, concentrate on getting back to the work at hand.

- Make a note (or leave a marker) where you were when you left off.

- Break your project down into steps. Interruptions are less disruptive if you're at a good stopping place.

- Even if you have to stop for an interruption, try to return to the task on which you were working.

4. If interruptions are still plaguing you, keep an "Interruption Log" for a week.

- After tracking where your interruptions are coming from, evaluate what you can do to reduce those that occur.

5. Learn to stop interrupting yourself.

- Create an environment that is conducive for the work you need to do. Remove distractions and have your supplies conveniently located.

- Set small goals with scheduled breaks (interruptions). As you begin to appreciate your new level of accomplishment, it will be easier to work for longer stretches of time.

- Don't start another project without finishing the one you're working on.

- Resist temptations that present themselves (drop-in visitors and the like).

- Don't procrastinate!

CHAPTER 18

• • • • • • • • •

The Two P's: Procrastination and Perfectionism

Procrastination and perfectionism: Have either of these time traps ensnared you? Mark yes for the items with which you identify; no for the ones that don't describe you.

YES	NO	
_____	_____	I put off dealing with my mail. When it arrives, I go through looking for the "good stuff," and somehow I never get back to it.
_____	_____	Reorganize my closets? They are a mess, but I just get depressed when I even think about it.
_____	_____	If I get a big assignment at work, it's so difficult for me to get started. I wait until it becomes a crisis.
_____	_____	I frequently find that my thoughts wander to other things, and I end up doing a different activity (catching up on my filing or skimming through a magazine) instead of the project I had intended.
_____	_____	I get hung up on making things right. I know

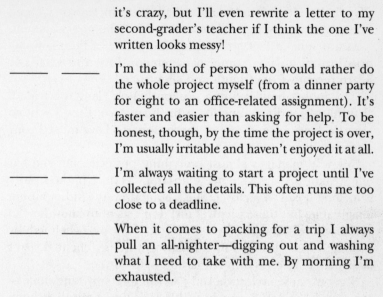

it's crazy, but I'll even rewrite a letter to my second-grader's teacher if I think the one I've written looks messy!

_____ _____ I'm the kind of person who would rather do the whole project myself (from a dinner party for eight to an office-related assignment). It's faster and easier than asking for help. To be honest, though, by the time the project is over, I'm usually irritable and haven't enjoyed it at all.

_____ _____ I'm always waiting to start a project until I've collected all the details. This often runs me too close to a deadline.

_____ _____ When it comes to packing for a trip I always pull an all-nighter—digging out and washing what I need to take with me. By morning I'm exhausted.

And what about yes or no to the two classic forms of procrastination:

YES **NO**

_____ _____ I wait until April to start filling out my tax forms.

_____ _____ I frequently finish my holiday shopping on Christmas Eve.

We all feel guilty when we procrastinate, but in reality, it's very much a part of human nature. What's more, an occasional bout of "procrastination-itis" is normal and even healthy. If it's a beautiful spring day, why stay inside and work when it would be much nicer to go out for a walk with your child or play some tennis? Depriving yourself of an occasional spur-of-the-moment activity would be unthinkable.

However, in many cases procrastination takes on a life of its own. Some people live in a constant state of procrastination; others fall into it temporarily. In the process of trying to control an activity by putting it off, procrastinators find that their action actually creates a heightened state of anxiety because they feel guilty for delaying and then begin to worry about when—and how—they will be able to fulfill their commitment.

As a matter of fact, procrastination is one of the main culprits leading to poor time management. Listen to what I've heard recently from friends and clients:

"No doubt about it. I'm a procrastinator," laughs a friend. "I think of sending someone a birthday card; then I wait so long I'd have to send one of those 'sorry to have missed your birthday' ones."

"My wife manages almost everything perfectly, but she has one weakness," says a client. "Our family's entire photo history is in shoe boxes in a closet. She's bought every kind of album imaginable, but those pictures just don't seem to know how to get in there by themselves. I think she's overwhelmed by starting." (As I listen, I'm wondering why my client doesn't take matters into his own hands and help out.)

"I get in these cycles where I just can't get anything done— at home or at work. Even when I have the time I misuse it," says another client in frustration.

"I'll admit it," says a friend. "I'm a perfectionist, and the more tired I am, the harder it is to let go. I'll just keep doing something over and over, trying to make it perfect."

If only people fully realized the price they paid in worrying about what they were procrastinating on (wasting time and energy in the process), not to mention the stress they suffer when the task in question must be done in a rush.

Perfectionists face a double burden. They not only have to do what they have planned out, but they either have to do it slowly to do it perfectly, or they have to do it over again if they decide their first attempt wasn't perfect enough.

As you can see, either time trap creates a painful way to live. This chapter examines how to overcome

- Procrastination

- Perfectionism

- How to help children avoid both

Procrastination

There are lots of reasons why we procrastinate. A task is overwhelming or too time-consuming. We'd rather be doing something else. We don't know how to do the task (lack the skills), or we don't know how to get started. Or maybe we suffer from poor work habits.

So we wait, hoping that the task will change, be done by someone else, or "go away." There are several basic steps you can take to help prevent procrastination.

1. Get organized. This doesn't mean spending days straightening out home or office; it means getting organized for the task at hand. For a new project you'll find that writing a list of the steps that need to be taken care of or collecting all documents in a file folder is often a good way to organize for the new task that awaits you. And remember, you don't need every detail to fall in place in order to get started.

2. Consider—and improve—your work environment. People often procrastinate because the environment is not conducive to getting things done. Of course you hate filing if your drawers are so stuffed that you scrape your hand getting files in and out, and no wonder you're late paying your bills if you have to comb the house looking for what you did with them each month.

3. Break large tasks into small steps. I've said this throughout— if you look at anything as a series of small steps, it won't seem so overwhelming. Have you ever watched a child eat a piece of the single-slice cheese by nibbling around the edges? That's what you need to do when starting large projects.

4. Start your day with your most difficult task. If you get that behind you, the rest of the day will be a breeze.

5. Make appointments with yourself. Nothing gets done if you don't set aside time for it. If you've been intending to take up landscape painting and have procrastinated for years, it's because you never made an "appointment" to do it. Start now. While fifteen- to forty-five-minute appointments are ideal for whatever you want to undertake, you can use as little as five minutes to assemble materials or research a good painting class—pick up the phone and make a few inquiries.

6. Seize extra moments. If by chance you find yourself with some extra time (an appointment is cancelled or someone is late meeting you), take advantage of the unplanned-for moment and get another step or two of a project taken care of.

7. Plan for leisure time and use it for leisure. Procrastinators frequently are hard workers, and sometimes they procrastinate because they feel they never get a break. If you get in the habit of scheduling leisure time and using it that way, you'll find you have less need to play hookey when you should be doing something else.

Now let's take a look at some of the classic types of procrastinators, and how their habits can be improved.

The "Accidental" Procrastinator

The Accidental Procrastinator puts off little things—responding to invitations, dealing with the last few pieces of mail, putting away the craft items their child used for a project. He or she is often a very good time manager in other ways, but eventually these little projects mount up. If you're an Accidental Procrastinator, take the following steps:

- Because the items being put off are small tasks, do as many as you can when they come up. Invitations should be responded to right away; filing a couple of papers can be done during a free moment; and the stack of mail should be completely taken care of every single day.

- Use deadlines to your advantage. When a small item comes up, set an artificial deadline. You'll find it much easier to get it done.

- Set aside twenty to thirty minutes daily for the "little stuff." By grouping miscellaneous phone calls or establishing a time when you take care of small details, you'll soon find that it's easy work to get done.

The Overwhelmed Procrastinator

At some time or other we're all Overwhelmed Procrastinators. Our plate is so full we can't decide where to begin.

"I'd just started a new job, and my boss became quite ill," says one fellow. "I hadn't a clue how things worked in this new place, and I was totally overwhelmed with how to keep my end of the department running."

"My husband got transferred overseas and had to go immediately," explains a client. "I was left alone with two children and a dog, and I had two months to figure out the details about moving to a foreign country."

- Ask for clarification or better instructions. People often procrastinate because something is unclear. The sooner you understand what you are to do, the easier it will be.

- Make a list of the steps (or various aspects) of the job. And break the project down, break it down, break it down. The job will become clearer and easier to handle.

- When you're overwhelmed, the most difficult thing is getting started. If the project is new or immense, and you can't yet define any steps, start somewhere—anywhere. If you jump in, you'll find that what you need to do will become clearer to you.

- Don't expect to have a major block of time when you can "really get going with this." Major blocks of time are very rare! Because you've broken the job into parts, it should be easier to find small chunks of time when you can do one or two things, working toward your major goal. I'll say it again: Even five minutes can be enough to accomplish something.

- Ask: "Is there a simpler way to do this?" Sometimes procrastinators take a roundabout route when there is a straight path.

- At the end of one work session, make a note of what you'll do next. If you've planned your tasks for the next time, you'll find that your desire to procrastinate will subside.

The "I Don't Want to Do This" Procrastinator

From calling for a dental appointment to diving into a volunteer project, there are many times when procrastinators delay, hoping that the task will go away or will be done by someone else. Of course, this rarely happens, and the "I Don't Want to Do This" Procrastinator ends up doing the dreaded chore under more stressful circumstances. The dentist is booked up, and you must take an appointment that isn't very convenient. The volunteer project still has to be completed, but it's done with lots of loose ends left hanging because of the lack of time.

Here's how to manage when you really don't want to do it:

- Ask: "What could happen if I don't do this?" If the consequences are negative (imagine having a cavity worsen or disappointing someone who is depending on you), it should spur you into action. On the other hand, maybe not doing it isn't so terrible. There are always some to-do items in your master notebook that have become less important. Yes, you were really angry that the town snow plow dumped a huge mound of snow at the bottom of your freshly shoveled driveway, but are you still convinced a letter of complaint is worth your time? (Best way to judge: Are you likely to gain anything from it?) Cross off all low-level priorities that you've put off doing.

- If you decide you must do it, is there someone to whom you could delegate the task? If not, take action on your own as soon as possible. You'll be amazed at how great you'll feel after putting it behind you!

- Find a way to make the task more pleasurable. Some people return telephone calls, listen to music or a book-on-tape while doing a boring household task such as ironing or polishing silver.

- Some types of unpleasant tasks can be accomplished during time you might waste anyway. One mother carries a bag with everything she needs for paying bills. "I write checks while my children are in dance class or karate. That way I never have to set aside time to do it at home."

- Recurring tasks that you don't enjoy (bill paying, filling out expense reports for work, etc.) should be written on your calendar so that you have a certain day devoted to taking care of it. Getting it done will become easier if you've established a routine.

- Build in rewards for yourself. If you're truly phobic about going to the dentist, promise yourself some small gift for making the appointment; establish a larger one for the evening after you've been to the appointment.

The "Last-Minute" Procrastinator

These are the people who claim they work best under pressure, who think they like the adrenaline rush when something must be completed by the next day. Yet it seldom works out the way they expect. I hear about it from my clients:

"I thought I could finish it in time, but I got a really bad cold three days before it was due, and there was no way I could work while I was sick."

"When we go on vacation, I always pack at about two a.m.," says another client. "By the time I get on the plane, I'm anxious and exhausted, and by the time the plane is taking off, I realize I've forgotten something."

Or: "I was so busy I couldn't shop before Christmas Eve, and by that time they had sold out of what my daughter really wanted."

If you're a "Last-Minute Louie," you know it. To reform, you must first *want* to live a different way. The client who wasn't able to surprise her daughter with that one dreamed-of holiday present was highly motivated to change, as was the fellow who got sick right before his project's due date. Maybe you haven't had a bad experience yet, but you know what those night-before jitters are like, worrying about whether or not you'll be finished, and if finished, will it be good enough? Here are some additional suggestions:

- Write down how working under pressure makes you feel. Does it keep you awake? Do you get an upset stomach? Are you tired afterward? Are you grumpy with your spouse or the kids? Or do you worry because you really didn't have enough time to do a good job? This should serve as a reminder as to why a change of habit is advised.

- Break your task up into steps with interim deadlines, and set your final deadline a day or two earlier than necessary. Then plan something fun for the day or night before the real due date. Now instead of sweating out whether or not you'll be finished, you can look forward to a lunch with a friend or a movie.

- Ask your spouse or a colleague to help you by taking a copy of your due dates and making you accountable. (Once you've changed your habits, this step won't be necessary, but it's a great way to bring about reform.)

Once you experience the pleasure of being able to relax the night before you teach a special seminar, leave on a trip, or celebrate the holidays, you'll never go back to your former lifestyle.

The Habitual Pocrastinator

The Habitual Procrastinator has made a habit of putting things off—studies show that twenty percent of American adults suffer from this malady. It's the most difficult kind of procrastination because the habits have become second-nature. Habitual Procrastinators have poor work habits and are easily distracted because they've never learned to settle down and get something done.

If you've fallen into the trap of habitually procrastinating, here's how to strengthen your self-discipline and sharpen your concentration skills:

- To change a habit, you must start with something manageable. Select a relatively pleasant small task on which you've been procrastinating. Establish the number of minutes you think it will take, and promise yourself to do absolutely nothing else with the time until you've finished the task. Don't take or make a phone call; don't touch an extraneous piece of paper. Do the task.

- If you've been procrastinating on something like exercising or cleaning a closet, chances are, you've been berating yourself for never getting around to these tasks. Make a bargain with yourself: You'll do it for no less than five minutes and no more than fifteen minutes on the first day. (Remember to break a task like closet cleaning down into small parts: straighten a shelf, sort through the twenty belts you have on a hook, etc.) This brief exposure will show you that performing the activity wasn't so terrible and that you made some progress. As soon as you take some positive action, your anxiety will disappear, and going back to it the next day will be less stressful.

- Refer to chapters 21 and 22 regarding a tidy environment. The Habitual Procrastinator frequently works in a cluttered environment where other undone tasks attract attention and take time when they shouldn't.

- If the telephone is your primary distraction, use a family member, colleague, or an answering machine to screen calls. If that requires more discipline than you have right now, work on your task in an environment where you can't be reached by phone—the public library, a conference room at work, or, in nice weather, the park.

Over time you'll find that you're less easily distracted and more capable of concentrating on the task at hand. If you find your poor habits creeping back, consider whether you're particularly tired or stressed. For a "refresher course," reread this chapter.

The Perfectionist

The Perfectionist is usually deeply attuned to how others view them. They want to do it "just right" so that they are above criticism. Unfortunately, this unrealistic expectation leads them into several possible traps:

1. Perfectionists give every task the same value. Having a pin-neat garage becomes as important as delivering a stellar proposal at work in an effort to land a new account.
2. They are indecisive. "I keep waiting for the perfect solution and then it becomes too late."
3. They delay. By not undertaking something until the last minute, they provide themselves with an automatic excuse as to why it isn't really perfect.
4. They start but don't finish. If they undertake something but never complete it, the project can never be judged as perfect or imperfect—and so they are "fail-proof."
5. They take forever doing a task, redoing it, and doing it again until it meets their unrealistic standards.
6. They do everything themselves. No one else can live up to these impossible expectations.

If you're a perfectionist, here's some helpful advice:

Make a list of the times in which your perfectionism most hinders you. Select just one area and work on tolerating less than perfect results.

Begin by trying to put projects in perspective. While your

boss may want the presentation materials for a sales meeting to be a hundred percent perfect, not everything in life deserves the type of tedious scrutiny that perfection entails. Must you really rewrite a thank-you note because the ink on two or three words smeared? The person will still appreciate hearing from you and, in all likelihood, won't even notice the smudge.

Ask: "How can this be corrected without taking up too much time?" A word processor lets you reissue a letter in a moment; correcting fluid lets you improve the look of a handwritten letter or envelope; glue can make the broken whole again. Evaluate whether there is a remedy to what's bothering you.

Know when to quit so you can move on. Unless you're going to lose your job over something, allow yourself only one or—at the most—two "do overs." After trying the third time to perfect something, quit.

Focus on results. Did your complaint letter (with a smudge on your signature) receive an apology from the company? Did a wrinkled suit prevent you from making that sale? Was your daughter fabulous in the dance recital even though her costume ripped and had to be pinned?

Don't be so hard on yourself. More often than not, doing a job that is good enough is perfectly acceptable.

Be open-minded. Sometimes you may even benefit from making a mistake. One woman who does public relations for a chain of hotels sent out an invitation to forty reporters, but the invitation lacked a date: "Lots of them called to find out when we were holding the event, and I was able to get to know some whom I'd never spoken to," she explains. "It seemed that people actually liked the very 'human-ness' of it, and as it happened, we had a much better turnout for the event than we had expected!"

The Apple Never Falls Far from the Tree: What We Need to Teach Our Children

One of the greatest gifts we can give our children is to help them develop good "lifestyle" habits. Youngsters who live in a chaotic atmosphere where things are frequently put off are less likely to create positive habits for themselves. Here's what you can do to help:

Even if you're a world-class procrastinator, you can help yourself and help your children by turning over a new leaf with items that come home from school. If a permission slip needs to be signed and returned by week's end, do it now and send it back the next day. If one of the classes is having a bake sale, write a note to yourself on the family wall calendar, reminding you to send the children in with some extra change for the bake sale.

Encourage advance preparation on all aspects of school work.

Make sure the house is well stocked with supplies. Younger children have a constant need for pictures from old magazines, poster board, and construction paper for projects. Keep age-appropriate items on hand so that they needn't delay getting started on something.

Teach children of all ages to break large assignments into parts. A child's first experience with test taking is generally the weekly spelling test, and this is where you'll begin to lay groundwork so that a child works nightly in anticipation of Friday's test. By reviewing with him or her throughout the week, you demonstrate that "cramming" on Thursday night shouldn't be necessary. As a child begins to face testing in other subjects, help plan out how to study so that a small amount of material is covered over several nights instead of one big push the night before the test. Or if your youngster needs to read a two-hundred-page book in a month and do a report, help him calculate how many pages per night he must read and still allow a few days to write the report. By teaching children this skill early you will have given them a tool they can use again and again.

A child's enthusiasm offers energy to anyone in the surrounding area. Whenever possible, act on a child's wishes as soon as you can. A daughter of a friend of mine wanted to shop for holiday presents the first week in December. "I had a million things to do," says her mother, "and this was not high on my priority list. However, I thought about disappointing her, and I realized we'd have to do it sometime. We made the few stops she requested that weekend. When she came home, even though she's only six, she wrapped everything herself, and I didn't have to do a thing. The best part was that she relaxed because she was finished, and that let me focus more fully on everything I had to do to get ready."

When Children Try to Be Perfect

Many children go through a stage when they try to be perfect—to do things "right." If this has turned into the never ending cycle of having to redo until perfect (accompanied by high juvenile frustration), then here's what to do:

Express interest in the process, not the product. Sit with your child while she practices scales on the piano rather than requesting that she play a finished piece. Compliment her on putting a lot of thought into her drawing or mention that you like the colors she uses. Don't stress success or failure of the final product.

Model a relaxed attitude. If cereal spills on the floor or the gift paper tears a little bit while wrapping a present, take a calm approach to correcting the situation. Showing that it's no big deal helps a perfectionist learn to tolerate small doses of frustration.

Talk about your own mistakes—current ones as well as ones you made growing up. If you view mistakes as learning opportunities, your child will begin to view them that way, too.

When a problem occurs, teach your child to ask: "Okay, but can it be fixed?" Children will sometimes throw away a drawing because the "dog's ears are too big" or wad up a paper because they made a mistake on their homework. The more often you are there to counsel that it can be fixed without starting over, the better off your child will be. Homework written on a word processor offers instant fix-it capabilities, but a pencil eraser or correcting fluid (even on a preschooler's drawing) can make life a lot easier for a child trying to do everything perfectly.

Show your child there are many ways to be "right." Sometimes children become very rigid about how a story must be told or the certain way a horse must look. Your own home library probably contains several books with horses in them. Show your child how artists have drawn horses in many different ways. And a librarian might help you pull several renditions of a popular fairy tale. After reading one of the traditional versions of *Beauty and the Beast* to your child, you might view the videotape, which adds characters and alters the plot line somewhat. It will help a young child understand that in life—whether you're telling a story, drawing a picture, or solving a friendship problem—there are many different approaches to take.

Checkpoint and Review

1. To prevent procrastination:

- Organize for the task at hand.

- Create a good work environment.

- Break large tasks into small steps.

- Start your day with the most difficult task.

- Make time to do something by scheduling appointments with yourself.

- Seize extra moments.

- Plan for and use leisure time.

2. "Accidental" Procrastinators should

- Do tasks as they occur.

- Set deadlines even when there aren't any.

- Establish a block of time to take care of the "small stuff."

3. The Overwhelmed Procrastinator needs to

- Get a clear explanation of the task and break it into parts.

- Jump in and get started.

- Find odd time and use it.

- Simplify the complex.

- At the end of one session, always prepare for the next.

4. The "I Don't Want to Do It" Procrastinator needs to

- Ask: "Do I really need to do this?"

- Act on it.

- Fit in undesirable tasks at odd or wasted moments.

- Schedule recurring tasks so that the routine aspect of it lets them get done.

- Establish rewards.

5. The "Last-Minute" Procrastinator can

- Set interim deadlines with an earlier than necessary final due date.

- Use a "buddy" system so that someone knows if you're staying on schedule.

6. The Habitual Procrastinator should

- Start with a small task and try to complete it without interrupting yourself or breaking concentration.

- Increase your expectations bit by bit, always working with one small step at a time.

- Create a tidy work environment to lessen distractions.

- Consider getting away from the phone by having a person or an answering machine screen calls; if this doesn't work, you may need to work elsewhere, in a phone-free environment.

7. To avoid perfectionism:

■ Identify one area where you can work on tolerating the less than perfect results.

■ Put life in perspective. What tasks are simply not worth doing perfectly?

■ Know when to quit doing things over.

■ Focus on results. Did you get what you needed from your accomplishment, even if some aspect of the project wasn't a hundred percent perfect?

■ Go easy on yourself.

8. To help a child avoid procrastination:

■ Set a good example with things that affect his or her life. For example, promptly process all school-related materials.

■ Have on hand materials needed for school projects.

■ Teach a child to study in small doses.

■ Capitalize on your children's enthusiasm. If they are excited about doing something, let them run with it. If they need your help, try to get around to it as soon as you can.

9. To nip childhood perfectionism in the bud:

■ Admire the process, not the product.

■ Model a relaxed approach to life.

■ Teach your child to ask: "How can this be fixed without doing it over?"

■ Show children that there is almost always more than one right answer.

CHAPTER 19

. . . .

The Two T's: Telephone and Television

"I don't know where the time went."

"I needed to get so much done this evening, and the time has just disappeared!"

Whenever I hear someone make comments like these, I know that, in all likelihood, the "time thief" was one of the two T's: the telephone or television.

Both inventions are wonderful, and both are time savers. The telephone puts us in instant communication with friends or family anywhere in the world, and makes it possible for us to instantly arrange for (or cancel) anything from movie tickets and dental appointments to the delivery of mail-order merchandise. We couldn't live without it.

The television brings the world to us. We see new movies, "Broadway" before our eyes, a baseball game that's taking place across the country, a film of an Antarctic exploration, and of course, all the national and international news. Previous generations never even dreamed of the possibilities of what could come to life right in our own homes.

But wonderful and amazing as they both are, they have another trait in common: They devour time and bring havoc to our schedules when uncontrolled. One unexpected phone call on your way out the door and you're late; a long-distance call when you're trying to put the kids to bed, and the evening careens out of control; or a momentary lapse when you meant to turn off the television, and the next thing you know you're hooked into the next program. . . . And then the one after that.

The answer to the "taming of the T's" lies in better management of both. This chapter will examine

- The telephone: General advice for home and office
- Telephone advice for the home
- Telephone advice for the office
- Maximizing your voice-mail system
- Television management

The Telephone: General Advice for Home and Office

Whether at home or in the office, each telephone area must be equipped with needed supplies. Have readily at hand:

- Notepad for message taking
- Pen or pencil. If your pens have a tendency to wander off, use one of the kinds that clip onto the telephone and has a cord.
- Area telephone book by each phone
- Your personalized phone book by the telephone used most frequently
- If you have difficulty reading small print, purchase one of the lighted "pocket" magnifying glasses and keep it by your phone book; you can read telephone listings without having to put on your glasses.

Keep a clock by the phone. Most people have no idea how long they spend on the telephone, and if you have a clock you can see conveniently, you'll begin to build an awareness.

Use answering machines or voice-mail systems at both home and office. You needn't miss the information the caller has for you, but you can screen out calls at times when you're busy with other things.

Group outgoing telephone calls so that you aren't always interrupting your day "to make a call," and make calls in order of priority.

Before you place a call, organize your thoughts so that you don't forget anything and have to call back. Focus on:

- Who you're calling

- What you need from that person

Establish at the outset of the call what your time frame is: "I'm leaving in just a few minutes, but I wanted to see if you knew any more about our plans for Friday?"

If your questions are going to take more than a minute or so, state: "I need a few minutes of your time. Is this convenient?" If the person you've called acknowledges that it is, he or she has committed to hearing you out. If it isn't, discuss when it would be good to call back.

If the person you're calling isn't in (and it's important to you to reach him or her), maintain control of the situation by saying you'll call back. If you've asked them to return your call and they don't, you may not make contact as quickly as you like.

Write down the results of your call in your master notebook and date the entry, including any details you'll need. If you've made a date to meet with someone, note the information in your planner.

If the call is for a specific reason, be certain you have your answer before drifting into a personal conversation with the person you've contacted. That way, if the doorbell rings or call waiting beeps one of you, you needn't call them back for what you needed.

When a call is dragging on, try some of the following lines:

- "What can I do for you?"
- "I don't want to keep you . . ."
- "I'm on my way out, but I have a minute . . ."
- "I'm working (or I'm busy with the kids) right now, so I've just got another minute . . ." (You don't really want to offer to call back.)
- "I have to go now, but please tell me about it when I see you on Sunday."
- "Before we end this conversation . . ."

Leave detailed messages to reduce future phone time. With voice mail or on an answering machine, you may be able to leave enough information that the party needn't call back: "I sent you the material you needed, so you should receive it Monday." If you will need to speak directly to the person, leave a message as to when it's easiest to reach you and also indicate you'll try again.

If you're concerned about the amount of time you're spending on the telephone, consider keeping a telephone log for a week:

INCOMING CALLS

Date	Who Called?	Why?	Time Spent	What You Were Doing Before Call

OUTGOING CALLS

Date	Called Who?	Why?	Time Spent	What You Were Doing Before You Called

Analyze your calling habits at the end of the week. The logs will provide you with a good idea of where you're spending the most time and when you tend to place calls. Are you originating calls that drag on, or are the people who call you interrupting what you need to do? Once you have an idea of what the problem is, you'll know whether you need to exert more self-discipline, or if finding a way to screen calls during part of your day will take care of the problem.

TELEPHONES THAT ADD CONVENIENCE

With today's telephones, you no longer need to have restricted range. Consider:

A cordless telephone. Perfect for use at home, these phones (with a range of a few hundred feet) permit you to sit on the deck and make a telephone call, or if you're rushing out the door, you can finish your call while letting in the dog and gathering your coat before saying good-bye!

A cellular telephone. These first became popular as car telephones (a great item to have in an emergency and a time saver when you're stuck in traffic) but are now used everywhere—on the street corners of major cities, in airports—anywhere people go, so go these phones. If you're inclined to try one, they do offer the advantage of instant access to family, friends, and colleagues without having to find—or wait for—a pay telephone.

Telephone Advice for the Home

On each telephone, tape a label giving your last name, house address, and the telephone number. In an emergency, a child or a flustered baby-sitter will be able to identify exactly where they are. Teach your child about 911 or whatever your emergency access number is locally.

Teach children exactly how to handle a telephone call, from whether they say "Hello" or "Smith Residence" to what they are to do when they need to call someone to the phone (Shouting into the receiver, "DAAAAD! It's for you!" is not the right answer). If your telephone has a hold button, teach them how to use it.

Near the telephone where you make most of your calls regarding family plans, keep copies of class and team lists (assemble them in a loose-leaf for a custom-made kid's telephone book) so that they are convenient for easy referral. If calls concern appointments affecting the family schedule, teach everyone to add items to the family calendar so that your schedule is always up to date.

If your children have a separate telephone line, invest in an answering machine to cover it. That way you're not in the kid message-taking business.

Establish telephone rules that are appropriate for your family. Some common ones you might consider:

- No telephone calls during dinner.

- Who answers the telephone in the evening? If the calls are primarily for your kids, ask that they answer the phone throughout the evening.

- If you have a business line in the house, are your children permitted to answer it? If so, how should it be answered and how should calls be handled?

- If you have call waiting and teenagers, discuss whose calls take priority. (In other words, express that they need to let you take incoming calls.)

- All messages must be written down; instruct family members to note down both the caller's name and telephone number so that you needn't look up the number once you get the message. Stipulate a family message center for putting phone messages so no one can forget to give it to the other person. (And be as serious about message taking for them as you expect them to be for you.)

SERVICES THAT SAVE TIME

Through the Telephone Company

Take advantage of the many telephone services that will help you save time. (Many home phone systems now have these services within the unit. See the next section.)

Caller ID (identification) is now available on phones you can purchase for your home. This will permit you to ignore calls from solicitors during dinner, but pick up quickly when your sister calls.

Call waiting. This service permits important calls to get through to you even when you or a family member are on the phone. If you leave a message for someone to call back, there's no longer any need to leave the line free until you hear from them.

Call forwarding. This service permits you to continue receiving your calls regardless of where you are—on vacation or at the neighbors. Although there will be times when you may prefer to have calls covered by an answering machine, it does permit you to forward and receive important calls, regardless of where you're going to be.

*66 and *69. You pay an additional fee for each time you use these particular services, but there are times when they can be worth it. Use *66 when you get a busy signal; the telephone company will keep redialing your number for up to thirty minutes until you get through. Dial *69 when you miss a call or when you realize you forgot to tell your previous caller something. The telephone company will redial the number of the last person to call you.

Through a Programmable Phone

If you haven't investigated "smart" telephones, you might like to do so. Depending on the model you select, they offer many conveniences. You'll find them with some, if not all, of the following features:

Speed dialing. You program in emergency services and your most frequently called numbers, and afterward you'll be able to call your best client or your mom by pushing only a couple of buttons.

Speaker phone. If you're on hold or on a long conversation, you can monitor the telephone or continue the conversation while your hands are free to do other things.

Redialing. When the number you've called is busy and you want to call back, you simply press "redial."

A "mute" button. You've taken a business call at home and your child has just entered the room, so you press "mute" until you explain to him that you're on a business call.

Conferencing capability. If you have more than one line, you can set up a telephone meeting by conference call. (This is especially convenient for teenagers—set rules on this, too!)

Intercom systems. If you have several telephone locations within the household, an intercom system is invaluable. No more screaming, "The phone's for you, Sam!", and because the intercom goes through your telephone system, the quality is much better than the style that plugs into an outlet.

Telephone Advice for the Office

If a secretary answers your telephone, he or she is your best ally against time-wasting telephone calls. Provide this staff member with:

- Information on solicitors and others from whom you never want to take calls

- A list of names of those from whom you will *always* take a call (family members, your boss, etc.)

- Permission to do as much legwork as possible before giving you the call. By asking what the call is in reference to, he or she may realize that this call can be better handled by a different department, and all of a sudden your latest problem has disappeared.

Prepare a frequently asked questions sheet so that the person who answers your phone has a good chance of being able to answer the caller's query.

Provide regular customers or clients with the names of other people in your organization who can help them if you're not in. This provides optimum service to your client, and it ultimately reduces your call-back list.

Let regular callers know when it's a good time to reach you. If you like to do priority work in the morning, let them know that you're generally available in the afternoon. And if you do not accept regular phone calls during certain morning hours, they'll soon find that it's preferable to follow your suggestion.

Office Message Taking

If a receptionist or secretary covers your phone, provide

accurate information as to when you'll be back, and if your schedule changes, call and notify them.

Never let a staff person say, "I'll see if she's in." This response implies that you're in to some but out to others. Remember, you've already provided a list of those you don't want to speak to, so an automatic "He's not in, but I'll leave a message for you" is sufficient.

If you can't take a particular call, give your secretary a time that you will return the call or can be reached. "Mary Ann can't take the call now, but does want to speak to you this afternoon. Can you call back at three?" Or, "Alan has meetings all day—he'll return the call first thing tomorrow morning."

Specify how you'd like to have your messages presented to you. Consider:

- Some people like a running log of all callers and their phone numbers. This provides you with a specific list from which to work, calling back in order of priority.

- If you need a record of all calls, you may prefer a carbonless message book. Your assistant fills out the "message" slip, giving it to you; he or she retains the message book, which provides a complete document of all incoming calls.

The old-fashioned spindle is great for holding message slips which can otherwise slide around and get lost among papers.

Save time by fax. Messages can be exchanged quickly by fax machine, preventing the possibility of being dragged into a personal conversation you don't have time for.

Voice-Mail Systems

Voice-mail systems are becoming as common as answering machines, though their capabilities are more impressive. With a good voice-mail system, you can send the same message to several voice-mail boxes; messages can be stored and retrieved selectively; you can add a beeper to the system for emergencies, and callers can leave messages twenty-four hours a day.

To maximize your voice-mail benefits, get in the habit of recording new voice-mail messages to keep them current. If you're taking a day off, the message should indicate you won't be getting right back to them. If you will be out of touch for a time, provide callers with another name to call.

If you have an assistant screen your voice mail, ask that a log of all calls be kept. He or she should "archive" (save) for you any that are very detailed or complicated.

If, in making a call, you encounter a voice-mail system, hit "0" if you want an operator instead of having to listen to a machine explaining an unending list of telephone options.

Always include in your message your name, number, the reason for the call, and when a good time to reach you would be.

Television Management

When properly managed, television is an asset in our lives. It's informative and entertaining, and brings most people great pleasure. The problem comes when it's time to turn it off.

Has TV Trapped You?

- How often have you fallen asleep watching television, only to waken with a stiff neck?

- How many times have you planned to watch a show and then accidentally left the set on, only to find yourself engrossed in the next program?

- Have you ever had company who turned on the television and the next thing you knew, all your guests gathered around the set to watch whatever was on?

- Have you ever had to delay dinner because a game ran over or a favorite television program hadn't ended?

- If you have children, do they often negotiate for a later bed-time in order to watch more television?

Your answers to the above will reveal whether you're controlling the television or if it's come to dominate your household. Here's what you need to do to put control back into your remote control!

The first step in better television management is evaluating how it affects your household. Ask all family members (you and your spouse included!) to keep a log of what they watch on television throughout the week:

TELEVISION LOG

Name _____   Week _____

PROGRAMS WATCHED	TOTAL TIME SPENT
Mon.	
Tues.	
Wed.	
Thurs.	
Fri.	
Sat.	
Sun.	

Evaluate what is important to you about television:

- Are you a TV news junkie? If so, what time of day do you prefer to watch it?

- List your three favorite television programs, and ask other family members to list their top three, too.

- If you use the television as background while doing other things, are there times when you find it distracting? (Do you ever stop your activity in order to follow the program more closely?)

Evaluate the practice of watching programs while doing other household tasks like fixing dinner. It may be perfect time management because you catch up on the news while preparing a meal, or you may decide that you'd rather listen to those language tapes you purchased a few months ago.

Consider your news habits. You may find extra time by reexamining what you're getting out of it. If you're catching the news at 6:00 P.M., you may decide to give up your ten o'clock news viewing and use the time for reading. Unless you change channels, many of the segments are the same anyway.

Instead of keeping a television log, some people like to break their TV habit by going cold turkey. After not watching any television for a minimum of a week, they find that it's easier to be selective about what programs they return to.

Changing Your For-Pleasure Viewing Habits: Appointment Television

You're going to manage your television time by using a new system: You're going to make an appointment to watch television. Examine both your television log as well as your answers to the questions concerning what aspects of television viewing are important to you. As a one-week experiment, write down on your day planner the times when you really care about sitting down to watch a program or moments when being able to catch a program makes a boring task you

have to do more pleasurable. (Combining dinner preparations with the evening news is a good example of this.)

If you have only one or two weekly series you care about
but do enjoy a lot of the specials, go through your favorite
television scheduling magazine. Have on hand a highlighter
and a 1″ × 1″ adhesive-backed notepad. As you read, highlight the programs that interest you, and mark the page with
notepaper. After reading the guide, add these programs to
your plans.

For a week, restrict your viewing to times when you've made
an appointment. Turn off the television as soon as your chosen
program is over. (This includes pushing the off button after
completing a chore you were doing while watching a show.) If
you're like most people, you'll be amazed at the time you save.

Take advantage of your videocassette recorder (VCR), an
invention that has greatly enhanced our ability to manage our
time and television viewing. If Friday night's regular program-
ming holds little interest for you, record and save a program
from Monday night to enjoy at your leisure. Or if you have to
do some envelope stuffing for a volunteer organization, record
one of your favorite programs and watch it while you get the
work done.

Although you needn't schedule by calendar in the future,
if you retain the concept of planned-for viewing, you'll
find that you've made smart choices and better managed
your time.

Just remember, if you're not watching television, turn it off!

DOUBLE UP: PLAN HOW YOU USE
YOUR VIEWING TIME

Although there are certain programs or times of day when
you just want to sit down and enjoy a program, it's also possible
to use television-viewing time as an opportunity to accomplish
certain tasks. By planning your schedule (and using the VCR),
you can arrange to catch up on your favorite programs while
doing any number of tasks:

- Stretching or exercising
- Grooming tasks such as putting polish on your nails
- Preparing meals
- Ironing
- Sorting receipts
- Addressing envelopes
- Knitting or sewing
- Cleaning out your briefcase
- Thumbing through catalogs
- Glancing through the newspaper

Family Television Rules

What Works

Set a limit on television viewing. Decide the amount of time you're comfortable permitting your children to watch television each day and then limit it to that.

Establish viewing rules. While some families permit a child to come home after school and relax watching a thirty-minute program before starting homework, other families stipulate that all homework must be completed before the television set is turned on. Even then the number of programs should be restricted to one or two favorites.

Give your children some control but stay involved. Permit them to specify what programs they want to watch. (With all ages, check the appropriateness of the programs they select.) If they have too many favorites on a given night, record the others on the VCR.

Teach them your highlighting system for the TV listings guide. A child who loves animals may find some terrific nature specials; a young ballet student will be amazed at the quality of dance available on television.

As often as you can, watch with them. Sharing and discussing a sitcom or a news special can constitute quality time. You'll be amazed if you listen to some of their comments and opinions on shows!

What Doesn't Work

Avoid putting television sets in your children's bedrooms. Once a set is in your child's bedroom, you relinquish the opportunity to monitor the time invested in watching. At its best, television viewing is a group activity in which several people can share and enjoy a program and talk about it later.

Under normal circumstances, prohibition of television watching generally doesn't work. (An exception is when the entire family decides to give up watching for a given period of time.) One mother explains: "I used to tell my children they couldn't watch television Monday through Thursday because of school obligations. What I found was that they were totally addicted once Friday came." Like other things, television viewing is best done in moderation. Having choice—with limitations—also teaches your child about self-control.

Checkpoint and Review

1. Develop a system that results in better management of telephone calls.

- Establish a telephone center equipped with pen, paper, and phone books.

- When you're busy, screen incoming calls.

- Group outgoing calls.

- Write down the results of important calls.

- When you make a call and fail to reach someone, leave a detailed message so that they either needn't call you back or so they know the best time to reach you.

- Keep a telephone log to track your calls and spot those that are particular time wasters.

2. Extend the system to be applied at home.

- Label your telephone with your name and address so that in an emergency, anyone knows exactly where they are.

- Establish appropriate telephone rules for your family.

- Take advantage of the numerous telephone services that provide convenience and save time.

3. Create a system for the office as well.

- Use a staff person to screen or handle as many calls as possible.

- Utilize other people in the organization if they can provide information for those who call you.

- If you're out of the offices, let the person covering your phone know where you are and when you'll be back.

- Select a message-taking system that works for you.

- Maximize your benefits from voice mail by changing the message when appropriate and getting back to callers promptly so they needn't call you again.

4. Work with your family on television management.

- Have all family members keep a log of their television viewing for a week.

- Evaluate your usage of television in the background. It may be the perfect way to keep up with the news, or it could be standing in the way of your accomplishing other things.

- Start setting "appointments" for your pleasure viewing.

- Use the VCR so that you can watch your favorite programs when it's most convenient for you.

- Maximize your time by planning to get some chores done during some of your viewing time.

5. Establish family viewing rules.

- Set limits on viewing without prohibiting television. (Practicing moderate viewing is generally more successful than advocating abstinence.)

- Let the children have some control over how their viewing time is used, but do check that what they select is age-appropriate.

- Teach them to use a viewing guide so they can find programs that appeal to them beyond the normal sitcoms.

- Watch with your children whenever possible.

CHAPTER 20

· · · · · · · ·

Losing Things

If you needed to, could you locate the following items you might have at home within five minutes?

YES	NO	
_____	_____	The telephone bill that came last week
_____	_____	The gift certificate you received for your birthday
_____	_____	A dictionary
_____	_____	The button that needs to be sewn on your jacket
_____	_____	Your child's permission slip she brought home Friday that must be returned to school on Monday

And at the office, could you find?

YES	NO	
_____	_____	A copy of a report you submitted to your boss a month ago
_____	_____	A business card of someone whom you met recently

_____	_____	Notes from a recent staff meeting
_____	_____	Your current expense record
_____	_____	Your to-do list

If you answered no more frequently than yes, you're in good company. People are forever misplacing things. Often they lose really important things like keys or glasses or birth certificates. Sometimes what they lose is less important (scissors, tape, the pen by the phone) but highly inconvenient to have misplaced.

Losing what you need causes lost time, because once you realize the item is missing, you have to spend time searching for it, sometimes endlessly.

What's the answer? You need to develop a system. As your life becomes more hectic, you begin to realize that trying to remember a lot of miscellaneous information (occasionally called telephone numbers or the whereabouts of the service guarantee on the vacuum) becomes less and less interesting. Why clutter your brain when a well-thought-out system could do the work for you? Here's what will help:

Establish a permanent home for anything vital to your day-to-day life. If you can't get along without it, then think carefully about the best location for that item. Here are some common examples:

- Glasses and keys should be kept in a logical place based on where you need them.

- Pen and paper should be placed by all telephones, in the kitchen, and on your nightstand. (If your pen tends to "wander away," then purchase a pen on a cord that fastens to the telephone.)

- A public-transportation pass should be kept in your wallet; tokens should have a container of their own near where you keep spare change. When you need more, you simply dip into your supply.

- Your hat and gloves (and those belonging to all family members) should be placed in a bin or basket near the front door or in the hall closet as soon as you arrive home with them.

- The dog leash should go on a hook near the door.

Other items should be stored so that there is a logic to it. If you use an item frequently, store it where it will be convenient. Infrequently used items should be stored on upper shelves or in the less convenient parts of cupboards, but label both the shelves (as to what belongs on each shelf) and the box or container (if the object is stored in one), and mark it so that the label is visible when stored. Pick up a label-making machine at a stationery store so that your labels are neat and easy to read.

Group items together by type (all large rubber bands together, all baking pans together) or by use (store together all gift-wrapping materials or all letter-writing materials).

Store according to season. Keep swimming gear together, winter clothes in one closet, etc.

Keep items near where they are used. Light bulbs for the dining room chandelier should be tucked away in a cabinet in the dining room. A dictionary and other reference books should be on a shelf near your desk. If you like to do crossword puzzles in the bedroom, then arrange to keep your puzzle book and pencil (and any puzzle reference books if you use them) in a drawer by your bedside.

Establish a table or even a basket near the door by which you usually leave the house for items you intend to take with you. This permits you—and other family members—to gather items like an umbrella or library books as you think of them so that you needn't hunt for them on the way out the door.

Teach family members to keep track of their own belongings. A spouse and children can create havoc in your life if you're constantly having to help them locate what they've lost. To help them:

- Assess whether there is any consistency to what they lose or when they lose it. Do they leave in the morning without everything they need? Do they arrive home from work or school, having neglected to bring home something important?

- Once you've evaluated what the circumstances are, you can then help them create a system that will provide a solution. One mother provided her son with a luggage tag for his backpack. Instead of name and address, she wrote in the window of the tag a checklist of what needed to come home from school. At home, kids should learn to make a list of last-minute reminders. Help them establish a place where they can leave notes for themselves about items they need to bring to school that day.

Teach family members to maintain your household systems. If they must borrow the kitchen scissors, then teach them the importance of putting them back.

The key to not losing things brings us to a very important rule of time management: *If you take something out, put it away.*

DON'T FORGET!

You can't do it if you don't remember it, and writing things down on little pieces of paper is not the way to go.

Write it down. Missing information will be missing no longer if you remember to take this first step: Put it in writing. Step two involves getting that information to the right place: Names and addresses should go in your address book or roll file. Some information belongs in your master notebook (see Chapter 3). Material for ongoing projects belongs in the appropriate file.

Have pads and pens easily available. If you have these in strategic locations, you can write down the thought when it comes to you and then transfer it into your master notebook when you have time.

Create a category in your master notebook where you can note down where you've stored items such as birth certificates or other important papers. When you need something and aren't quite certain how you categorized or filed it, all you need to do is consult your notebook.

Keep lists of everything from "questions to ask the doctor" to "things to pack for our vacation" in your notebook. Use your notebook for running thoughts on everything going on in your life right now.

Use adhesive-backed notes for up-to-the-minute reminders. If you're doing some desk work and want to be reminded to make a call at three o'clock, stick a reminder to your phone. Do you want to be sure to remember to take your brother's sweater with you so that you can return it to him today? Put a note on the kitchen counter or the back of the door.

Mind over Matter

Establishing systems is a giant first step toward developing a lifestyle that will help you keep track of things. In addition, try these "mind" tricks:

Slow down. Most of us spend a lot of time in life's fast lane. The phone doesn't stop ringing; the requests from family or co-workers becomes a barrage; the doorbell rings unexpectedly—no wonder we misplace things! The cure is to slow down. If you've just removed from your file the warranty for the refrigerator repairman, and the doorbell rings, focus on the fact that you have it, concentrate on holding onto it or make a mental note of where you put it down. (And when you originally pull it from the file, put a reminder note that you removed the warranty on a certain date and took it to your desk in the kitchen. If you forget to refile it, your reminder will give you a clue as to where to start looking for it.)

Create an image of where you put something. Let's suppose you're hiding a birthday present from your inquisitive spouse. The only problem is you're worried that you'll hide it too well. Try "imaging." If you concentrate on really looking as you put something away, that same mental picture will return when you need to retrieve the item. If visual imaging doesn't work for you, try using other senses. If you're storing something in the basement, there is likely a distinctive smell of dampness, or if you're placing an object on a rough surface, the feel of the rough shelf might be what you remember. Focus on how it feels or smells as you put something away. You might even try rhymes. If the special present is a hat that you're hiding in the basement near the sports equipment, you might try: "The hat is with the bat."

Announce to yourself where you are putting something: "I'm putting my glasses on my kitchen desk." This type of verbalization can be a great help in locating items that typically move with you from place to place (glasses, current reading material, etc.).

If You're Misplacing Lots of Things, What Does It Mean?

Can you identify with these four people?

My friend lost her address book (no backup copy) when they were renovating her home: "I had it in my hand when the contractor needed me. I tore up the three rooms we were living in looking for it, but it never showed up."

"I brought my wife home from the hospital after surgery, and later I couldn't even find my coat! Our routine was different as we came in, and I was just totally stressed," explained a client.

"The new baby must have had magical powers and spirited away our belongings. There's no other explanation for the number of things I misplaced after coming home with our second child!" remarked a former neighbor.

"My husband had been very ill, and I went to the gym just to burn off nervous energy," said a friend. "I took off my mother's watch, which I dearly loved, and left it in the locker but forgot to lock it up. When I returned, it was gone."

What these four people have in common is a high level of stress. If you find that you're misplacing a lot of things (your watch, calendar, plane tickets), then before worrying about the missing items, see if there's anything you can do about your stress level. Try:

- Temporarily reorder your priorities so that you can forget about some responsibilities for a little while.

- Ask for or hire help.

- Go for a walk or do something that pulls you out of the stressful environment for a time.

- Take a nap or just sit down and relax for ten minutes.

- If you're overextended and can't see when there will be any relief, try to address the stress head-on. At work, talk to your boss. Together the two of you may be able to come up with a reordered plan so that you accomplish your priority work without feeling so much pressure. If the stress is home-related, sit down with your spouse or a friend. He or she may have suggestions on how everything might be managed better.

The Three Most Frequently Lost Household Items and How to Keep Track of Them

I visit many houses, and here are three frequently misplaced items and some advice on how to keep track of them.

Keys

If you've tried to establish a set place for them and it isn't working, then you have to start fresh. Buy a special bowl (or put up a hook), and make a rule for yourself: Keys are either in the bowl (or on the hook) or in your purse or briefcase. Even if you dash into the house to answer the telephone, don't permit yourself to put down your keys until you've put them in one of those places!

Losing keys is a real inconvenience and source of worry (can't lock up, can't drive the car), so be a realist. Have copies made. Keep an extra set in a safe place at home, and give another set to a neighbor. (Don't write your name or address on the set that goes to your neighbor. If their house is burglarized, the crook may realize he now has keys to yours.)

Glasses

Ideally, you want to establish a specific "home" for your glasses, preferably near where they are most frequently used, but glasses are difficult because you may be anywhere when you decide to take them off. Try choosing a "glasses resting place" for each room in your house. Even if you have to do a room-by-room search, at least you know there is only one place in each room where you need to look. (Make it a safe place on a specific shelf or table; don't ever leave glasses on couches or chairs.)

You might also consider wearing your glasses on a chain around your neck. That way you're not leaving them behind as you move from room to room.

Like losing keys, it is very upsetting to lose glasses; always have a spare pair on hand. (Take the spare when you travel. There's nothing worse than being away from home without glasses and an easy means to replace them.)

The Pen by the Phone

How often have you tried to leave a telephone message for someone only to have the person on the other end of the conversation say, "Just a minute, I can't find a pencil"? Then you wait while a search is conducted, and by the time they've returned, you're beginning to wonder if leaving the message is worth it.

We can make our own telephone message centers more efficient by:

- Using a pen-on-a-cord system so that the writing implement can't "walk"

- Keeping a pencil holder filled with writing implements. If you have eight to twelve pens, pencils, and markers available, chances are very strong that you'll have something to write with when a phone call comes in.

Other Items You Hate to Lose

Gift certificates	Place in your bills and receipts file a special envelope labeled "Gift Certificates." When you're planning an expedition to that store, you'll know just where to find the certificate.
Theater tickets	Store these in your tickler file (see Chapter 15) under the appropriate month (or date, if you've done a day-by-day system).
Favorite letters, souvenirs	Create a memory box so that you'll have a logical system for putting away things that are important to you.
Important papers	Keep these in a well-thought-out filing system.
Lists	These belong in your master notebook.
Non-grocery coupons	Coupons for the grocery should be stored in special wallets they sell for the purpose. (Look through any housewares catalog to find one.) Store non-grocery coupons right here along with the coupons for the grocery. That way you have all coupons together in one place, and you'll always know where to find them.

Telephone numbers	When someone gives you a telephone number, enter it into your address book or your roll file right away. That way you'll have it when you need it.
Your money	In the morning, check how much money you have and sort it by denomination. At the end of the day, recheck the amount you have left so that you know how much you spent that day.

Checkpoint and Review

1. Develop thoughtful systems for putting things away.

- Establish permanent homes for must-haves like glasses and keys.

- Keep items near where they are used, and store frequently used items in the most accessible places.

- Teach family members to keep track of their belongings and to maintain your household systems.

2. Don't expect to remember everything.

- Write notes to yourself in your master notebook.

- Keep track of where you've stored important items by writing it down in your notebook.

- Keep pads and pens in all the logical places so that even when you're not near your notebook, it's easy to write something down. (Later it should be transferred to your notebook.)

3. By concentrating on what you're doing, you'll find it easier to retrieve what you've put away.

Use visual images and the spoken word to impress upon your memory where you've put something.

4. If you're losing more things than usual, chances are it's because you're experiencing a lot of stress.

Ask for help or try to cut back temporarily.

5. Establish systems for keeping track of the most frequently lost household items.

CHAPTER 21

• • • • • • • •

Neatness Counts at Home

In my profession I've seen just about everything. I've been led through mazes of paper and magazines in homes and apartments. I've seen bedside tables piled so high with paper and mail and books that any sleeper should fear for his or her life. I've seen closets stuffed with everything, including old peanut butter sandwiches. I've also been to homes that looked great— but no one had a clue as to where things were stored. The putting away had been delegated to someone who never considered setting up a useful system.

Household chaos is a classic time trap, because it reduces anyone's ability to manage time. How can you leave the house promptly if everything you need is scattered about? And as for doing anything—from wrapping a gift to cooking a meal—that requires space and supplies, it's simply imperative that you have a well-ordered place with the things you need nearby.

Are you in control of your environment? Answer the following questions:

- Could you sit down and read a magazine without having to move things off the couch?

- Are your kitchen counters clear enough that you could fix a meal without having to rearrange or do the dishes first?

- In your closet, could you pull out any item of clothing, knowing that it's been hung neatly and is clean, ironed, and ready to wear?

Neatness can create a more orderly state of mind so that you feel in control of your time, not trapped by the circumstances that arise in a messy environment. If you strive to have a home where you can move about efficiently and not have to worry about locating things, you'll find that managing your time—and your life—becomes much easier.

One warning: This isn't a one-time fix. Maintaining a more orderly environment requires constant diligence. If you continue to work at putting things away and neatening up as you go, you'll notice a slow but steady change in the way you live. One day you'll be expecting company, and you'll look around and realize that at last you don't need a week's warning so that you'll have enough time to pick up!

This chapter will highlight what you need to do to be able to find what you need when you need it. You'll learn new systems to live by as I take you through:

- The general household

- The kitchen

- Closet management

THE TEN MOST COMMON THINGS PEOPLE ALWAYS LEAVE OUT

1. Money
2. Mail (opened and unopened)
3. Keys (house and car)
4. Clothes, shoes, jewelry, gloves, and coats
5. Toys

6. Books and magazines
7. Lists
8. Photographs still in the folder
9. Food
10. Things they want others to deal with

New Systems to Live by

Everything must have a place. Sounds simple, doesn't it? But you need only stroll through your house to realize this isn't an easy task. At home where should you put:

- Birthday gift for party four days from now?

- Mantel clock that needs to be repaired?

- New clothing that you haven't had time to try on at home yet?

- Forms for Little League registration on Saturday?

It's generally the items that are "just passing through" our lives that people have trouble putting away, and yet that's exactly what creates a clutter build-up. After a time that birthday present you left out gets buried under a pile of suits laid out for the cleaners, and the next thing you know, the bow is flattened, and when you're ready to leave for the party, you determine that the gift is "lost."

The only way to remedy the situation is to find a "home" for each item that enters your house—even those that come in temporarily. Establish a way station near the door for items due to depart soon—the cleaning, the birthday gift, the mantel clock you're taking to the clock maker on Saturday. Clothing you haven't tried on yet should be hung in the closet. The longer it stays folded in the bag, the more wrinkled it gets, and if you decide to keep it, you'll then have to take time to iron it. Important papers that need to be sent out should be placed in a file for the next day's to-do work and should receive priority treatment. Once you get the hang of it, you'll find that assigning logical storage for everything isn't as difficult as it sounds, and the benefits of clutter-free space will make the effort worth it!

The success of this new state of organization depends on one more system:

Keep up so that you won't have to catch up. This means:

- If you take something out, put it away. If you take something off, hang it up. If you drop it, pick it up. If it doesn't belong where it is, put it back. If you make a mess, clean it up.

- Stay on top of chores or paperwork.

- Don't procrastinate, or your to-do list will multiply before your eyes.

The General Household

Make a practice of always putting away whatever you bring home. Put away all groceries, drugstore purchases, dry cleaning, and find a special spot for those books you picked up at the library. If you make this one simple change, you'll begin to streamline your life.

To work on household improvement, you can create a list of the areas that are in the greatest state of chaos, and face them in order of priority. Another way to do this is to write the areas of the household requiring neatening up on slips of paper. Put the slips in an envelope clipped into your master notebook. When you've got an extra twenty to thirty minutes, draw out one of the papers and do twenty minutes of de-cluttering in that area.

Eliminate everything you don't use. Don't bother to organize what you don't need.

Save on cleaning time by rotating some of the items you keep out on display. If you move them around and put some of them away for a time (in labeled boxes that should be stored in the attic, basement, or on a top shelf in the closet), you'll find that you appreciate them more as they appear in different locations, and it reduces the amount of time you spend cleaning around them.

Reconsider the purpose of each room and make the household more convenient by storing items near where they are used. If you rarely have time for doing puzzles anymore, then you might consider moving puzzles out of the family room cabinets and down to the basement to make space for the games your family is currently enjoying.

Group like items together (a real time saver) in the area where they will be used:

- Gift-wrapping supplies, complete with scissors, tape, and pen, should all be stored near a surface where you can do the wrapping. Don't forget to add some all-occasion gift cards and enclosures—they'll come in handy.

- Buy a plastic caddy at the hardware store and use it to hold cleaning equipment for general household cleaning. For more frequent clean-ups in the bathroom, keep cleaning supplies, a sponge, paper towels, garbage bags, and rubber gloves (if you use them) under the bathroom sink so that you needn't run all over for the equipment you need.

- Reference books such as an atlas, dictionary, and thesaurus should be stored near your desk or near where your children do homework.

Children's rooms will be easier to maintain if you keep them current. If Jimmy no longer plays with his blocks, this is a good time to move them out of his room. If Maggie prefers to play in the family room with her friends, you might consider whether or not the dress-ups in her room might be kept downstairs instead.

With a family, household clutter can be impressive. Use a basket (or if the children are old enough, ask them) to go around picking up all the items that are in the wrong rooms. Then go back through the house with the basket, putting away all items where they belong.

Family members can help save time by practicing better household management:

- Starting when they are very young (one and a half isn't too early), encourage children to put away what they take out. The bonus is they'll find it again. When children three and a half and older refuse to help with clean-up, bring out a big garbage bag and suggest that you will have to throw out or give away what is left out. Clean-up will be faster than a magic wand!

- Teach everyone, including children five and up, to write items on the grocery list when you are low, not out.

- Establish a family message center where phone messages and other family notes can be left.

- Create a kids' telephone book by buying a 1" ring binder to hold all your children's class and extracurricular-activity telephone lists.

- Provide each child with a folder for important papers. Set up a spot for these folders. It is the perfect place for the permission slip to be signed or for little ones who want you to look over their homework.

- Even the youngest family members will keep a neat closet or bathroom if you provide ample hooks, drawers, and shelves low enough for them to reach so that they can hang up clothes, hats, and robes, and store shoes, slippers, and bathroom toiletries.

Leave a room better than you found it. Put away the magazines you were reading, but also take time to straighten the couch pillows and fold the blanket the kids were using. (Better yet, have *them* fold it!)

The Kitchen

When it comes to time management, there are two major problems with getting things done efficiently in the kitchen:

1. When people move into a house, they settle into the kitchen *once*. Though their lifestyle may change, they don't consider reorganizing their kitchen to make it work better for their new needs.
2. The counter work space is often so filled with things that there isn't enough room to work.

Here's what you need to do to make your kitchen work for you:

Assess your space and consider who uses it. Do the kids like to do homework while you're in the kitchen? Has your teen become an avid cook, so you need to be certain there's work space for two? Do you need a mini-office in the kitchen?

In general, kitchens need the following work centers:

- Food preparation and cooking area

- Serving area (place where plates can be spread out)

- Space around sink for unwashed dishes

- Baking area

With these thoughts in mind, consider what you can do to reorganize your kitchen to better utilize the space you have. Your kitchen will be more convenient if:

- Items used together are stored together, and they should be stored near where they are used. Everyday dishes should be stored near the sink or dishwasher. Ready-to-use food such as cereals should be stored near your food-preparation area. Baking utensils and ingredients should be in cupboards near your baking center.

■ And remember, don't store what you don't use—give away the dishes you haven't touched in over a year (finest china and items handed down to you by Grandma not included).

Many people stack things to maximize storage, but retrieval of these items becomes awkward and slow. Stack obvious items like plates or infrequently used dishes, but try to create a separate place (no stacking necessary) for items like a pot or serving dish you use several times a week. This will simplify getting it out and putting it away.

Putting away your groceries in a thoughtful order will make it easier for you to locate what you need when you need it.

■ Group all food by type (cereals, soups, pasta, etc.).

■ Label shelves as to what belongs where.

■ Alphabetize items you have in quantity, such as spices, soups, and canned goods. (This is smart time management, even if others chuckle.)

Your refrigerator management should also be efficient. Establish certain shelves for certain foods and group like items. Items used most frequently should be stored on the door or toward the front of the shelves.

Date and label baked goods and leftovers as well as anything you freeze. (No more time wasted peeking into those aluminum-wrapped surprise packages!)

Closets

How many days a week do you waste time digging through closets for one thing or another? Whether you're searching for the gray slacks you "know" came back from the cleaners or for your son's baseball mitt or for the other glove you need now that the weather has turned cold, this is time you could save if you make your closets manageable.

If you're like most of my clients, your clothes closet isn't the only closet in need of a redo, so establish a cleaning-out schedule you can live with. Can you attack one closet per weekend? Two closets per month? Decide what is realistic for you and write it down in your master notebook. (Family members over age ten should be involved in working on their own closets. If they will help you elsewhere in the house, enlist them!)

Whether it's the front hall closet or your clothes closet, the process is the same. Every closet should have a light to enhance visibility. Walk through your house and note all closets that don't. It's worth the added cost of having one installed to be able to see what is in your closet without struggling.

Take everything out of the closet. If that alone will create havoc because there's so much "stuff," divide the closet into thirds, removing all hanging items first, then all items on upper shelves, and finally evaluating what is currently on the floor.

Vacuum, wash down, and then apply—or have someone do it for you—a coat of polyurethane on all closet shelves. It will speed any shelf clean-up. Most polyurethane applications dry very quickly, so by the time you've finished sorting things, your shelves will be well on the way to being dry.

Sort through your belongings and create four piles: Yes, No, Maybe, and a Store Someplace Else pile.

1. The No items should go directly into boxes or bags for their next destination, whether it's passing things on to cousins or taking them to a charitable organization.
2. Maybe's are those items you're not sure fit (or if they do, do they flatter?). The family member to whom these items belong should set aside time to try them on so that

an evaluation can be made. (Maybe's that remain questionable—does it really look okay?—should go into the No pile. Rarely does age improve their status.)

3. The Store Someplace Else pile may consist of out-of-season clothing that can go to another closet or the attic. It may be clothes one child has outgrown but that you'll store in the basement for his or her sibling. It may be that old clock you put on the bottom of your closet, thinking that one day you'd have it repaired. (Now is the time to pass it on or have it fixed; don't store what doesn't work.)

4. Your Yes pile should be put away neatly.

As you put items back, pull out anything that should be cleaned or repaired, and group like items (shirts with shirts, trousers with trousers, etc.).

As you work, keep asking:

- Are the most frequently used items at eye level and near the front of the closet?

- Can I see everything easily? (Don't store things behind other things.)

- Can I reach what I need quickly and with a minimum of effort?

Don't store clothing in dry-cleaning bags. They block your vision and may actually cause damage to the clothes.

If space is at a premium in your home and you need to use upper closet areas for regular storage, keep a footstool in the closet so that it takes only a minute to get down anything that's up high. Items on shelves can be stacked, but don't make the piles too high. It becomes cumbersome to remove something on the bottom, and items stacked too high will keep toppling over.

Stumped by what to do with all the things you no longer use, have outgrown, or don't want to be bothered with? Have one big tag sale and profit from your cleaning out. You'll be amazed at how valuable your rejects can be to somebody else.

THE NEATNESS CHALLENGE

Go through your home, room by room, and list every item you left out or forgot to put away. For each item set up the following two columns and put a check in the column that best explains why the item wasn't put away:

Item	Didn't Know Where to Put It	Just Didn't Bother To Put It Away
1.		
2.		
3.		
4.		
5.		

Did you need more than one sheet of paper to make a complete list? (If so, you're in serious need of reform! Reread the chapter.)

How many checks do you have in Column 1? Checks in this column mean you need to work harder at finding convenient places to store things.

How many checks do you have in Column 2? Lots of checks here mean you need to exert greater self-discipline.

Checkpoint and Review

1. An orderly environment saves you time because you know where things are and have put what you need where you need it.

■ Everything must have a place.

■ Keep up with putting away so that you won't have to catch up.

2. Around the house:

- Always put away what you bring home.

- Eliminate what you don't use.

- Group like items together when you store them.

- Teach family members strategies to help with household clutter and keeping track of their things.

- When you leave a room, leave it better than the way you found it.

3. The kitchen:

- Keep your counter space as clear as possible.

- Store items near where they are used.

- Avoid stacking dishes for easier retrieval.

- Date and label baked goods and leftovers (particularly those that go into the freezer).

4. Closets:

- Install a light in every closet.

- Clean out closets and sort through your belongings.

- Have a coat of polyurethane painted on to all closet shelves to make for easier cleaning.

- Give away anything that hasn't been worn or used in a year.

- Don't put away anything that needs to be cleaned or mended.

- If you have to stack clothing like sweaters or towels, keep the stacks low.

- Profit from your clutter with a big tag sale.

CHAPTER 22

• • • • • • • •

Neatness Counts at the Office

A television producer of a popular national show loved her job and was very skilled at keeping track of the hundreds of details involved in producing the program. "Juggling is my specialty," she once told me. What her job responsibilities didn't allow time for, however, was keeping a neat office.

One day she was stunned when her boss commented on how disorganized she was. "If I was disorganized, I couldn't get the show on the air," she fumed.

Her chaotic work space was an indication to her boss—and others—that she was operating "out of control." Despite her very efficient job performance, her messy office painted a devastating image of herself.

While a messy desk doesn't necessarily bring on a pink slip, it is often a symptom of disorganization. You can check how important this is in your department or company. What does your boss's desk look like? If he or she keeps things tidy, you better clean up fast!

And if you think it doesn't matter because you're self-employed, it does. I know from visiting countless offices that people waste an average of thirty to sixty minutes per day "prospecting" for the various papers they need. There's no doubt about it. A messy office or desk wastes time.

To find out how badly you need help, answer the following questions:

YES   NO

——— ——— Do you frequently find your eyes drifting from your work to the other things that are parked on your desk?

——— ——— If you go through your to-do stack right now, will you find things that you should have dealt with several days or weeks ago?

——— ——— Would it take you more than five minutes to look for a document you need immediately or that someone has requested from you?

——— ——— Do you often come up blank when trying to figure out where a piece of paper should be filed?

——— ——— Within the past month have you seen the surface of your desk—clear and dust-free?

If your office is on the brink of disaster, now is the time to gain more control. This chapter will help you bring order to chaos by examining new systems to live by that will help you manage both

- Your office
- Your desk

IS WHAT YOU NEED WHERE YOU NEED IT?

To test whether or not you're set up for maximum efficiency, answer the following: When you're at the office and sitting by your desk, what do you have within arm's reach?

- your master notebook
- your calendar
- your address book/roll file
- letterhead stationery
- envelopes
- note paper
- desk accessories (stapler, tape dispenser, etc.)

New Systems to Live by

Maintain a clean desk. The only items that should be on the surface of your desk are your desk accessories and the project you're working on. To achieve this, make it a goal to clear your desk every night before you quit working.

Process everything that comes into your office on the day it arrives. Holding on to mail or memos is a guarantee of an office flooded with paper.

Don't accept what you don't need. If papers that would be better handled by someone else arrive in your office, forward them immediately. You don't have to process what isn't there! One executive takes his own notes at meetings so that he doesn't have to bother with other people's notes or reports.

Your Office

"I panic when someone calls and needs information," says one client. "I'm always afraid I won't be able to find what I need for them when I need it."

When I visit offices, I see a never ending stream of clutter.

Because our work lives have been speeded up by fax, e-mail, and computer, it seems there is less and less time spent managing the real work that needs to be done. Most business people could add valuable time to their day if they would de-clutter their offices and set up a streamlined environment. This would entail eliminating unnecessary paper and reducing what was on hand to only what was needed.

The person with a cluttered office may, indeed, be able to find exactly what he's looking for, but he's using a lot of energy trying to remember where the "papers for the Smith Account" are. He could be using that energy for other things like finishing a report or preparing a speech or taking care of the little things that mount up over time. He's also taking a risk that he really will be able to locate the papers needed. Consider how much easier it would be to simply file things under "Smith."

The well-thought-out office is comfortable and convenient and conducive to work. To find out how yours stacks up, perform an "office check-up" and modify any aspects of your office that aren't in "good shape."

Are you distracted by people walking by your door? Position your desk in the center of the office with the doorway to your side. That way you'll be in a good position to welcome visitors, but you won't be constantly aware of the passing parade.

Are you plagued by drop-in visitors? If so, you may need to replace a comfortable chair with a style that's less welcoming. Investigate wooden chairs or director's chairs—comfortable enough for an appointment, but not the kind of chair anyone would want to stay in for too long.

Do you frequently run out of office supplies? If so, set up a system for your office. Put a clipboard in the closet or cabinet where supplies are stored, and as soon as someone opens the last box of pens or paper or copier fluid, they should note on the list that a new supply should be ordered. An employee should be assigned to check the list weekly so that the office is aware when you are low, not out.

When you're at your desk, are your files close by? Frequently used files should be in the file drawer of your desk or in a file cabinet within easy reach. (Some people have lateral files right behind their desk, meaning that files are accessible with a swivel of the chair.) If file cabinets are far away, I find that people just keep everything on their desk. It's a mess!

Are you drowning in paper? You need to make time to weed out. You don't need most of what you think you do. As a general rule, you can eliminate a great deal of what's on your desk and in your files.

If some of your mess is inherited from the person who held the job previously, you need to do two things:

1. Spend time getting to know the files. People may call your office looking for things you didn't even know you had.
2. Earmark items to go to dead storage. If you're new in the job, you may not be knowledgeable enough about what to eliminate and what to keep, but by getting it sent elsewhere in the building, it will free space in your office.

Is your wastebasket convenient? It should be. The more you throw away as you go through the mail and old files, the less time you will have to spend managing it.

Do you have shelving, and if so, what are you storing there? Shelves should be for books and binders. Too often they become the home of stacks, which are a very inefficient way of storing anything. Stacks of paper should be reviewed and placed in separate files where they can be stored in a dust-free filing cabinet and retrieved when needed.

How is your office lighting? If you're working under fluorescent bulbs all day, you might like to add a desk lamp to provide incandescent task lighting. Reading and file retrieval is faster because you don't have to strain to see.

Your Desk

"I don't have time to straighten out my desk. I have too much to do, and it just ends up a mess again," complain many of my clients.

"Make time," I tell them. "You need a system, and you can do it by devoting only fifteen minutes a day to the process. It's the single biggest time saver you can give yourself."

Here's what I suggest:

The Fifteen-Minute Plan

Start with the tallest pile on your desk, and begin working through it, evaluating each piece of paper and what to do with it. Make one of the following three choices:

- *Toss.* Unwanted mail, memos, and papers that should have been responded to but are now too old should be placed directly into the recycling bin.

- *File.* Papers that need to be kept should go directly into the proper file. This should be done easily if you followed the earlier advice to put your files within easy reach of your desk.

- *Respond.* If a simple response on the bottom of a letter or memo will suffice, then do it during your fifteen-minute work session. If the response will require more time, place it in your collection of materials for what you intend to do tomorrow. Write down what you need to do on your to-do list.

At the end of your fifteen-minute session, stop working. (Your recycling bin should be overflowing, and your pile

should be considerably smaller.) Take a look at your calendar and schedule in another fifteen-minute block of time
tomorrow.

Keep working for as many days as necessary to get your desk
down to the bare surface. Your goal is to achieve a clean
desk with space for the following:

- Blotter

- Telephone

- Answering machine, if this is your choice for message
  taking

- Clock

- Calendar

- Address book or roll file

- Pencil holder containing pens, pencils, scissors, ruler, and
  letter opener

- Paper clip holder

- Stapler

- Tape dispenser .

These items are generally used daily, so they should be kept
within easy reach.

Now that your desk is clean, you're ready to practice desk
management. Create three file folders to help with managing
incoming papers.

1. "To Copy" file. Jumping up and down to make photocopies is a waste of time. If you need a copy of something, place it in this folder. Delegate the copying if you
can. If you can't, do your own copying at a time of day
when the copy room is quietest so that you don't have to wait
in line.

2. "To Enter" file. People are always in need of entering information into their computer. The best way is to save items throughout the day and do it all at the same time. As you come across financial statistics or names and addresses you want in your computer files, put the paper into this file. Then schedule time at the end of the day for making the entries.

3. "Take Home" file. Some people like to keep their brief-cases close by and simply put papers directly into the case. Others prefer placing papers in a file that gets transferred to the briefcase at the end of the day.

Files are an important key to office organization. Every time you start a new project, reach for a folder and label it for the new project. Even a project that must be completed in a day requires a folder. Afraid you'll forget about it once it's filed? With your new time-management system, you'll write the project down in your master notebook and break it down into the steps you need to take to complete it.

An In basket and an Out basket are great ways to manage paper flow, but place your In box on your credenza or on a shelf near the door rather than on your desk. (Or ask that people leave papers and messages in an envelope-style pocket mounted right on your door.) If you have a direct view of the incoming work, it can distract you from the project at hand. (And no, it won't be within arm's reach, but you'll maintain control of your paper by handling it when it's convenient for you.)

Set aside regular time for doing paperwork. Come in early or stay late and have your telephone calls screened for a period of time so that you can keep up with the paperwork that, if permitted, is capable of swallowing up your desk.

When it's time to focus on your incoming paperwork, handle each piece of paper quickly and efficiently. Also, refile what you take out.

Checkpoint and Review

1. New rules to live by:

- Keep your desk clear so that you can work in an orderly environment.

- Process what comes in every day.

- Don't accept papers you don't need.

2. Your office:

- Create an environment that is conducive to work by evaluating the positioning of your desk.

- Store near you supplies and files you use regularly.

- Try to manage your papers effectively. Toss out as much as you can and file the rest.

- Have a wastebasket near your work area.

3. Your desk:
Attack your desk in fifteen-minute blocks of time. Work through your piles and toss, file, or respond.

4. Develop systems that make paperwork easy.

- Manage active papers by creating and using three file folders: To Copy, To Enter, and Take Home.

- If you're starting a new project, create a file for it right away.

- Set aside regular time for doing paperwork.

- *Always* refile what you take out.

Section 6

· · · · · · · · · · ·

SPEED TIPS AND SHORTCUTS

CHAPTER 23

. . . .

170 Ways to Do Things Better

The key to better time management is setting priorities and making the best use of the time available to you. However, it doesn't make sense not to look for the fastest and easiest way to accomplish many routine tasks. This chapter offers speed tips and time savers for the following tasks so that you'll have more time for what you really want to do:

Car time
Children
Commuting
Cooking
Desk work
Entertaining
Five things you can do
   in five minutes
   in ten minutes
   in thirty minutes
For the self-employed

Gift shopping
Grocery shopping
Grooming
Holidays
Household chores and
   maintenance
Laundry
Meetings
Reading
Travel
Wardrobe management

Car Time

While in the car, your life can be more comfortable if you don't have to search for what you need:

- Avoid a car key hunt. Everyone in the household of driving age should have everyone else's car keys. Color-code using nail polish; pick up some of the off-beat colors to code according to the color of the car.

- Establish a special place for keeping keys. (See Chapter 20.)

- Buy a visor organizer (available in auto-supply stores). Use it to store extra change for tolls, gas and toll receipts, and a small pen and pad of paper.

- Clean out your glove compartment! It should include automobile and important information, auto insurance card, security cards, emergency telephone numbers, emergency money (change and bills), and a mini-flashlight.

- A roll of paper towels, a box of "wipes," tissues, extra garbage bags, a portable umbrella, and an imperishable snack could come in handy—particularly if you have children. Store in a box or container that's out of the way but still accessible.

- Put a laundry basket (or large plastic tote basket) in the back of your car. As you do errands, all packages go in this single receptacle. This will save time by reducing the number of trips you make carrying packages from the car. It also prevents packages from rolling around while you're in transit.

- Keep records of car maintenance so that you get your car serviced regularly.

READY FOR FUN

If you visit a beach or pool regularly, keep a tote bag permanently packed with beach towels, sunblock, T-shirts, sunglasses, reading material, and beach toys for children.

Restock after your day in the sun.

Children

As your children become more independent, you'll find that you need to invest less time in maintenance chores, and you'll have more time for the fun part of parenting. To help guide them:

- Help children help themselves. Purchase small pitchers for milk and juice, and keep them on a lower shelf of the refrigerator, and always have healthy snacks readily available.

- Fold and store outfits together—a real time saver when searching for matched sets. As they get older, show them how to do it for themselves.

- Teach young ones the valuable lifelong habit of keeping like things together—from stationery to toys to athletic gear. That way they'll find it when they need it!

- If your children are driving you crazy (and they are old enough not to need constant supervision for safety reasons), send yourself to your room for ten minutes, announcing that you'll be in a better mood after you chill out for a few minutes. And guess what? You will. A few minutes of reading, meditation, or closing your eyes will make you feel better. By the time you return, the children will likely have calmed down, too.

- Do you want to instill organizational skills in your children? There's no better way than setting a good example. Children learn by what they see.

ASSUME NOTHING

Always confirm appointments;
don't assume the other person will remember.

Commuting

Most of us spend some portion of our day getting to and from work. Here's what you can do to maximize the time you spend.

- If you live in a densely populated area, start your commute to work earlier than you used to. You'll be traveling when traffic is lighter, and the bonus is that you'll have some quiet time at work.

- If you're not too far from work, walk or bike. The time doubles as great exercise time and a quiet time to think.

- If you take public transportation, your commute time is golden. Many people do work-related reading and planning on the way to work and use the ride home to relax, read, play cards, or do crossword puzzles. Bus riders often get off a few stops early to get some errands done or enjoy a brisk walk.

- If you drive, consider carpooling with a carefully selected group of people. Invite on-time friends with whom you'll enjoy sharing the ride.

- If you drive alone, you can catch up on radio news or enjoy books on tape. Those who get started listening to books find it addictive!

- Keep a small recorder in the car so that you can dictate notes to yourself.

- Used judiciously, a cellular phone saves time while driving (and offers enormous benefits in an emergency). If you're running late or want to confirm an appointment, you needn't go in search of a pay phone. However, reserve your calling for times when you're stalled in traffic, since statistics show an increase in accidents for those who phone and drive.

- Investigate whether you can work from home one or two days a week. This saves commuting time, and you'll find that you use your time at the office and your work time at home more effectively, for you'll understand the benefits of each.

Cooking

Everyone has to cook. Although there are times when you want to take time to prepare a special meal, there are many days when streamlining will be a great help.

- Cook in quantity. Schedule a cooking day every other week or so, and make and freeze several casseroles for nights when you don't have time to fix dinner.

- Prepare healthy foods such as a large fruit or pasta salad that will last a few days and that the family can dig into.

- Dovetail tasks. If you're having vegetables as a side dish on Monday, cut up extra for Tuesday's stir-fry.

- Make good use of prepared foods. If you're making stew, buy meat that has been precut. If it looks fresh, pick up pre-washed lettuce. Pre-cooked lasagna noodles make life a lot easier.

- The longer dirty dishes sit, the more time it takes to clean up. Fill sink with soapy water so that as you cook, you can soak pots, pans, and plates immediately after use.

- "Clean up as you go" is also good advice for counter spills. The more quickly you mop up the excess tomato sauce, the less time it will take.

- Order in or eat out occasionally—the best time-saving tip of all!

STAY IN CHARGE

When the person you're trying to contact isn't in,
try to get the information from someone else.
If no one else can help you, stay in charge
by saying you'll call them.
That way you won't be left hanging.

Desk Work

Desk work at home and office needs to be made more efficient. Give these tips a try.

- Don't share frequently used items. Buy scissors, pens, and tape dispensers for any room in the house where someone might use it. It's a waste of time to be ready to wrap a package, only to discover that the tape and scissors are missing. And if family members or co-workers do borrow something, remind them to bring it back.

- Buy a rubber stamp or an embosser with your return address on it.

- Buy prestamped envelopes to make letter writing and bill paying easier.

- Buy stamps in quantity, and keep extras on hand. Order by telephone and save time (1-800-STAMPS 24).

- Send postcards instead of letters.

- Use the photocopy machine judiciously. Always ask: "Do we really need this copy?" Creating more paper for you and others to manage is a tremendous time waster.

- Insurance forms take a lot of time. Partially complete one health insurance form for each family member and photocopy it. Then add pertinent details after each visit.

- Photocopy your credit cards so that you have a quick way to report a loss.

- List your various insurance policy numbers and family members' social security numbers in your personal phone book so that you'll have them when you need them.

Entertaining

Who has time to entertain? You do.

- Have one big bash instead of small parties.

- Or have two parties back to back. This maximizes the time you've spent cleaning the house, arranging a centerpiece, and getting out special dishes for entertaining.

- Entertain for brunch, not dinner.

- If dinner is your choice, plan potluck. You'll save time and have more fun if everyone participates.

Once your guests have been invited:

- Divide and conquer. Make two lists: a do-ahead list (buy paper goods, imperishables, etc.) and a last-minute list (timetable, cooking chores, final house straightening, etc.). Give yourself deadlines and delegate chores to others.

- When preparing hors d'oeuvres, consider doing double and freezing one of the trays for another night.

- Keep a to-do list in the kitchen during any party. That way when you're refilling the hors d'oeuvres plate and talking to someone, you can still grab a quick look at what needs to be done.

- Start a party file. Keep an invitation list, menus, and post-party notes on what you would do differently.

TIME SAVER

*If you don't know how to do something,
ask someone who does.*

Five Things You Can Do in Five Minutes

1. Sort the mail.
2. Clean out your purse or briefcase.
3. Send a postcard to a friend.
4. Return one phone call.
5. Write tomorrow's to-do list.

Five Things You Can Do in Ten Minutes

1. Skim the newspaper.
2. Go through a stack of papers and take care of at least five items.
3. Plan a week's worth of dinner menus and write the ingredients on your grocery list.
4. Catch up on filing.
5. Put away laundry.

Five Things You Can Do in Thirty Minutes

1. Go through five sets of old photos. Sort, date, and place in an album.
2. Reconcile your checkbook.
3. Clean out your medicine supply cabinet, tossing dried-up creams and anything with illegible labels or instructions, or medicine that is older than its expiration date.
4. Read from your on-the-go reading file.
5. Watch the television show you prerecorded last night.

BE PREPARED

Always have your master notebook or a small pad and pen with you for taking notes.

For the Self-employed

Working for yourself is a blessing and a challenge. On one hand, you have all the time in the world. On the other, if you don't manage it carefully, your business is lost:

- Get up and dressed early, as you would if going to the office. You'll be more productive.

- Have a business line and personal line with answering machines. Monitor, but don't regularly answer, your personal line during business hours.

- Have a work schedule and stick to it.

- Schedule an established time for meeting with customers or clients, and group the meetings that occur.

- Schedule two business lunches a week so that you stay in touch and don't feel isolated.

PRACTICALLY SPEAKING

Ask the store to assemble anything that must be assembled. Unless you or a family member are skilled in that department, it will waste your time.

Gift Shopping

Shopping for gifts can take time if you don't plan ahead. Here's how to be prepared:

- Organize a wrapping-paper center. Establish a shelf or a drawer, or purchase a large plastic organizer to keep the following: wrapping paper (birthday, new baby, anniversary, and all-occasion), tape, packing tape, string, ribbons, tags, and bows. Buy all-occasion cards and gift enclosures as well. Pick up some decorative bags for the hard-to-wrap item. (You can take advantage of seasonal sales since you've already established a place to store these things.)

- Establish a gift drawer or shelf where you can tuck away gifts you've purchased in advance or items you love and want to use for small, occasional gifts.

- Pick up gifts as you see them. You'll select very thoughtful items because you have the time, and you'll avoid last-minute shopping for birthdays or the holidays.

- Take advantage of sales at toy stores to stock up on birthday presents for your children's friends during the coming year. Buy multiples of anything that you think is really terrific.

- Limit your shopping to one store. For example, at a bookstore you can find something to fit everyone's taste.

- If you can't decide between two gifts for someone, buy both and save the second one for their birthday or the following year.

- For friends or relatives who live far away, try to shop at stores that will wrap and mail the gifts. (Save on time and save on sales tax!)

- Wrap gifts as you buy them. Use an adhesive-backed note to label what it is and who it's for.

- Don't have time to shop?

  - Whenever possible, shop by mail or phone and have gifts wrapped and sent.

  - Personal shoppers (at most major department stores) will shop and send for you if you provide a description of the person and a price range.

  - Send gift certificates for special treats: movie tickets or video rentals, a facial, a session at a favorite beauty salon, dinner for two at a special restaurant, or a club or museum membership.

  - Give a personal IOU for a task to be done (run errands, fix a meal, clean a closet); give food baskets. Keep extra jams, special vinegars and mustards on hand when you need to bring a gift and don't have time to shop.

  - Keep a list of your gift giving throughout the year, and file each year's list in a Gifts file. Then when you want to know if you already gave a set of handkerchiefs to Uncle Harry, you'll have an easy way to check.

FEELING UNDER THE WEATHER?

When you're at the doctor's, have a nurse call in the prescription so that you don't have to wait at the pharmacy.

Grocery Shopping

Stopping at the grocery store several times a week for forgotten items is a colossal waste of time. Grocery shopping is tailor-made to be routine. Here's how to establish a system:

- Create a shopping list (according to the layout of your supermarket) of all items you regularly purchase, and photocopy it. (Why originate the same list every week?) Family members can check off what is needed that week or add in something special.

- Make a list of your everyday meals, and note the ingredients needed for each one. Use it to help create your grocery list.

- Shop monthly for all grocery store basics. Your weekly trips are then reduced to just enough time to pick up the perishables.

- If you have the storage (basement? garage?), buy in bulk: toilet paper, soap, toothbrushes, grooming supplies, tissues, shampoo, shaving cream, razor blades, as well as imperishables like cereal, powdered milk, drink mixes, and mix desserts.

- At the store, help pack your own groceries so that you can pack together items that are stored together—all frozen foods in one bag, extra paper goods for the kitchen in another bag, etc.

- Save time later in the week by organizing your groceries (and preparing some items) as you put groceries away:

  - Make fresh juice.

  - Wash and cut up fresh vegetables.

  - Mix up fresh tuna fish if that's a staple in your household.

  - Divide meat into appropriate portions, label, date, and freeze.

  - If you pack lunches, prepack snack-size portions of what you'll need later in the week.

TIME AWARENESS

*Have a clock in every room. By remaining
aware of the time, you'll use the time you
have available more wisely.*

Grooming

Grooming is a daily task in which you can save time by being
organized:

- Keep all hair, skin, and makeup supplies on a convenient
  shelf. Store them in the order you use them.

- Establish a time length for your getting-ready routine so
  that you'll know if you're running ahead or behind.

- Streamline your cosmetics by using multi-function products
  such as foundations that contain sunscreen or moisturizer,
  or a cheek highlighter that doubles as a lip color.

Holidays

When it comes to the holidays, the most important time-
saving tip is *simplify*. All the complex festivities require time
and drain energy, depriving us from enjoying what is really
important—friends and family.

- Really large families frequently draw names for gift giving.
  That way each person is responsible only for one other
  family member and can devote time and money to getting
  just the right gift.

- Select a play or performance and buy tickets for family and
  friends. It offers a pleasurable activity for all to do together

in celebration of a holiday. (Some families use such an activity to replace gift giving to an ever expanding list.)

- Stock up on batteries at sales throughout the year. By December you'll have plenty for your children's toys and other gifts that require batteries.

- Invite friends or relatives over to help with tree decorating or baking. It provides you with extra hands at the holidays, and at the end of the day all the cookies are split among the participants.

- If your children are eleven or older, delegate some of the responsibilities to them. They love being in charge of baking and wrapping, and older teens can even be responsible for getting the tree and setting it up.

- Carry a few holiday cards and envelopes with you. Whenever you have to wait for an appointment, you can write a card or two.

- Buy ornaments, lights, wrapping paper, and decorations right after Christmas. Avoid having to rush out to buy these things in the crunch of the following December, and save money at the same time.

Household Chores and Maintenance

No doubt about it, household maintenance takes time. Follow this system to make it easier:

- Clean out regularly. Last season's clothes, gifts you never liked, books you'll never read, need to be moved around, cleaned around, and managed. Weed out your possessions, and you'll find you'll enjoy what you own even more.

- Rooms look better when they are de-cluttered; take time to put away and straighten up every day.

- Always leave a room better than you found it. This not

only reduces the number of heavy cleanings, but the job will be faster and easier.

- Keep a basket at the bottom or top of the stairs. Drop things into it and grab it when you're ready to make the trip.

When Cleaning

- Devote twenty to thirty minutes in the morning and the same amount in the evening to keeping up with cleaning chores. By keeping up, you'll find it less necessary to catch up, wasting a whole day on Saturday.

- Do deep-cleaning one item at a time. Clean out one cupboard, dust one set of bookshelves.

- Do two things at once. Have the scouring powder working in the tub while you're shining the bathroom mirror.

- Concentrate on cleaning at eye level, spending less time where no one looks.

- Try to do tasks in bulk. Iron only once a week or so.

- Do tasks that you're in the mood for. Cleaning out a drawer or straightening a table can be enormously satisfying, so capitalize on what you feel like doing.

- Know when to quit. Just because you cleaned out a cabinet doesn't mean you have to do three drawers as well. If you get things done in twenty-minute spurts, the task does get accomplished and you don't feel resentful.

- Carry a basket with you for collecting items that are in the wrong rooms. Redistribute later on.

In the Bathroom

- Keep cleaning products in the room where you use them.

- Wipe up daily to make weekly clean-up faster.

The Laundry

A never ending chore. Here are a few tricks of the trade:

- Keep a spray bottle of stain treatment near each laundry basket so family members can treat their own clothes before putting them in a hamper.

- Keep up with the laundry. Most households usually need to have at least one load per day running; get family members to help you fold and put away. If you use a laundromat, go on off days at an off hour.

- Stock up on socks and underwear for the family so you never *have* to do the laundry. You can save time sorting by having a specific style of sock for each child (white anklets for one daughter; white ribbed for another; dark socks for your son, etc.) and wash each style in individual mesh laundry bags. Sorting time will be reduced because you'll know right away which socks are whose.

- Eliminate other hand laundry by using a lingerie bag and washing on gentle cycle.

- Fold your clothes immediately after they come out of the dryer to reduce ironing time.

- Keep several pre-threaded needles handy for sewing on a loose button or stitching a torn hem.

- Have a basket for dry-cleaning so that there's a place to put it.

CAN'T WE DO THIS BY PHONE?

If someone calls for an appointment, see if the matter can be taken care of on the phone.

Meetings

If you're scheduled to attend a meeting:

- Note in your planner what time you need to leave for a meeting in order to be on time.

- If it's a long meeting covering several subjects, see if you're needed for the full time.

If you're holding a meeting:

- Hold them only when absolutely necessary.

- Schedule breakfast meetings. They are shorter and people can take action the same day.

- Try a "stand-up" meeting—they are usually very brief, productive, and results-oriented.

- Prepare a written agenda so that people come prepared.

- Delegate note taking so you know that it's done.

- Have index cards on hand at the meeting so that everyone can write down their notes or assignments.

Reading for Fun and Business

Even people who like to read sometimes have trouble finding the time. Here's how you can make reading a priority and make good use of the time you have for it:

- Schedule regular reading time daily or weekly.

- When you sit down to read something, consider how much time you really need to give it. If it deserves a skim, give it a skim.

- If it's something important, select a time and a place to read it where you won't be distracted.

- Have a highlighter and pad and pen close by. You can highlight a magazine article or a business report, or make notes if reading from a book.

The newspaper could take up all day if you let it! Here's a speedier way:

- Go through each section of the paper in order of importance, scanning for what interests you. The headline and the first paragraph will give you the basics of most stories.

- Read the stories that are important to you in greater depth. Most articles provide "past history" as you get toward the end, so you'll find it's a rare article that you need to read from start to finish.

- If an article is interesting but not vital, ask yourself, "Do I have time to read this today?" If you do, read and enjoy it. If you don't have time, clip the article and file it in your On-the-Go Reading file to read at a later date.

Business reports are important but can be tedious. Here's what to do with each one:

- Give it a quick glance. Should you read it immediately, or can it wait? If it's important, write it in your master notebook. If not, put it in your reading file.

- Look for logical breaks in what you're reading, and skim the material so you'll know what you're looking for.

- Read the first and last paragraph of what you're reading. This often summarizes what you'll be learning about.

If you enjoy novels or relish settling in with a good magazine, make it part of your daily routine:

- With both books and magazines, scan the table of contents. A magazine's table of contents will tell you which articles you're interested in reading. With a book, the contents will provide you with a guide as to where the book is going.

- If you're having trouble finding time to read a novel or nonfiction book, establish goals for yourself: perhaps three chapters per week. The more you get involved in the book, the easier it will be to find time!

- Reconsider your magazine subscriptions. In all likelihood, you're getting ones you don't need.

CHECKLISTS, CHECKLISTS

Make up checklists for recurring activities (travel, packing, meetings, sales calls), so that nothing is overlooked.

Travel

- Have an on-the-go toiletries/cosmetic bag that's packed and ready at all times. Why waste time repacking trip staples like toothpaste? When you get home from a trip, restock the bag before putting it away.

- Try to pack lightly enough that you don't have to check your bag.

- Put items you don't want to forget in a specific place during the week before you leave. It saves running around the house the night before you go.

- If you travel frequently, investigate the different guidebooks and select one brand that you like. Then whenever you're planning a trip, you'll be familiar with the guide's format and will find it easier to follow restaurant suggestions, hotel recommendations, tour itineraries, etc.

- Prepare your itinerary (and be certain everything is confirmed); check in frequently at the office.

- Before leaving, create a to-do list for your return.

- Use your airline ticket folder to store receipts so you can summarize your expenses when you get back.

- While away, have your mail routed to someone who can sort out and dispense with as much as possible. If on a business trip, have some sent to you so that you won't return to a backlog.

IT'S ALL IN THE BAG

Invest in one terrific all-around handbag with lots of compartments for organizing your belongings. Avoid the daily drudge of switching your gear from one bag to another.

A Woman's Wardrobe

"I have nothing to wear!" means spending time *looking* for something to wear. Here's what to do:

- Always have one perfect outfit hanging in the closet.

- Limit your wardrobe. Fewer choices saves time.

- Choose clothes in a coordinated color scheme so that you'll have more mix-and-match items and your shoes and handbag are more likely to coordinate.

- Buy easy-maintenance clothing whenever possible.

- Pick up the accessories you need at the time you buy an outfit.

- To keep your closets pared down, make a rule: When you buy something new, go through your closet and make certain that something goes out.

- Organize your closet by category and color so you can find things quickly.

- Store your jewelry neatly, according to what you use most often. Put earrings in pairs and detangle necklaces. When you want to get dressed, you'll find you can do so in half the time.

- Dress in front of a mirror so that you can catch anything about your appearance that needs correcting: Do you have a run? Is there a loose thread on your jacket? By catching it early, it allows you to cope before it's too late.

- Use a shoe polish sponge to spot-shine shoes before you put them away. They'll be ready to go the next time you decide to wear them.

NO? NO? YES?

Don't ever take a no from someone who does not have the authority to give you a yes.

Section 7
• • • • • • • • • •

Conclusion

CHAPTER 24

. . . .

Staying in Control and Enjoying Your Found Time

Now that you've read *The Overwhelmed Person's Guide*, you should have a good idea of where your time goes and how you'd like to be spending it. In reading the book, you will have learned a host of helpful time-management skills, and you'll recognize a time trap when you see it.

"So now I'll never be overwhelmed again" I hear you saying.

Of course you will! You're only human. Everything will be fine, and then you'll catch a cold right before you're leaving for vacation, and the first thing you know, you've got too much to do, and too little time.

Or you'll find yourself facing a new undertaking without an inkling as to how to get started. Four days will go by, and you'll realize you're procrastinating!

This is when *The Overwhelmed Person's Guide* becomes a trusty handbook. Turn down corners, use a highlighter to underscore helpful advice, and write in the margins if you have some personal notes to add.

You *will* get overwhelmed again, and the solution is to go back to the book and reread the sections where you need some additional help. Caught by a web of too many errands? Reread that chapter to get going. Drowning in unopened mail (from just the past three days!)? Do a check-up on your mail-handling habits. Having trouble with interruptions? Help is at your fingertips.

Always remember:

Setbacks are a part of life. Take it in stride, and regain control of your time as soon as you can.

The only real mistake you can make after reading this book is to encounter a setback and give up.

Now and then I'll have a client whose attempts at time management are constantly challenged, and so he'll become discouraged. "No one understands *my* time management problems . . ." "This will never work for *me.*"

Giving up is your only enemy.

You've read the book—you know we talk about everything from planning and priorities to time-management emergencies and the battle to minimize interruptions. The skills taught in these pages can and do work—they have to because they offer the only time-management remedy there is; there isn't any other secret. You can't expand your day. All you can do is decide carefully how you're going to spend it.

As we've discussed, when people begin feeling overwhelmed, one of the first things to go by the wayside is leisure time to spend with friends or family or just to enjoy on your own.

I'd like to leave you with some ideas of what you can do now that your current demands are better managed. (And if you still don't feel you have leisure time, look again at your priorities.) Life without some fun built into it is drudgery. Carve out time every day to do something pleasurable that's just for you.

Joining the "Leisure Class"

As you become better at building some leisure time into your schedule, you'll actually find it rejuvenating. By taking fifteen minutes to play checkers with your child, twenty minutes to read a novel, or thirty minutes to go for a walk with a spouse or a good friend, you'll soon find that by letting the pressures lift briefly, you'll be better prepared for managing day-to-day stresses.

For Body and Soul

Just as you take care of others—be they family members or fellow employees, you need to take care of yourself. Some of the best ways involve doing things that are good for your body that you also enjoy:

- Hop on a bike. Go alone if your lifestyle is one in which you're always surrounded by people. Take a friend or a spouse if you never have time with them.

- Go for a swim; line up a golf game or a tennis match. Pick your favorite sport and find someone who shares your passion. If your first few times together are fun, set up a regular schedule so that it becomes something you can look forward to.

Taking a Broader View

Or develop activities that broaden your world. Try anything that lets you see things differently.

- Get tickets for a concert series or the theater, or a professional sports team's hometown game. (If you know you'll like it, commit to a season ticket; you deserve to do something you enjoy more than once!)

- Take a day trip to a neighboring community; enjoy a leisurely lunch and a stroll around town.

- Try a new hobby. Most adults have something they've been meaning to try if only they had the time. Well, now is your chance. Set aside the time and try it!

- Join a book club (book clubs for couples are a growing trend).

Couple Time

If it seems you and your spouse conduct all discussions on the run, renew your commitment to "couple" time. Consider:

- Do you need one-on-one time? Establish a tradition of Saturday morning breakfast together (if you have kids, feed the kids separately), book a "date night," or find time each weekend to share a hobby.

- Has your couple social life been lackluster? Schedule some dinners out with friends, or invite some people in. If you're a gourmet cook, you may love fixing a meal; if you're not, bring in Chinese food, or ask your guests to bring a dish. Everyone faces the same time problems you do, and they'll be delighted to contribute to something fun.

Family Time

If family time is what's missing, make a point of guarding the time you have:

- Look at your calendar and decide which evenings can be established as family dinner nights, when all family members are home and can eat together.

- Encourage kids of all ages to help you so that even if you have to get something done (fix dinner, do dishes), you can spend that time talking or just being together.

- Establish time before or after dinner when you can devote a little while solely to each child. (Guard their right to you by screening telephone calls with an answering machine.) If they don't need help—or mental support—while doing homework, plan something else you can do for twenty to thirty minutes.

- Read to them until they are so old they rebel (then suggest they read to you!).

- Grab "teen" time when you can—in the car or at 10:30 P.M. when they are finally ready to talk. And remember that the offer of a good lunch out on a Saturday afternoon is rarely refused.

Never underestimate the importance of this time. Whether it's spent talking, reading, hugging, or listening, it will become your most profitable investment.

Personal Time

Pamper yourself. Women might consider the following activities:

- Sign up for an exercise class or make an appointment for a facial or manicure. Do something that's just for you.

- Plan a monthly get-together with other women for dinner or make arrangements for regular bowling games or a night out at the movies. Life is a lot more fun when you're sharing it with a group of people you enjoy.

Men might like the opportunity to:

- Grab some extra time on the weekend for practicing a favorite sport.

- Take an afternoon to go wherever you want to whether it's up to the lake for some fly-fishing, to a neighboring town to look at antique cars, or to the city to see a new art exhibit, make it time that's just for you.

These are just a short list of the rejuvenating activities each of us might pursue. When you think of the pleasure you could derive from adding even one of these items to your life, it should reinforce your determination to keep your priorities straight.

When you find the demands of life becoming overwhelming, review what's really important to you. We each have 24 hours in every day. Make the most of yours.

You can do anything, but you can't do everything.

The ultimate success in time management is knowing that you accomplished your top two or three priorities for the day and still had time to do something *just because you wanted to.*

The effort you put into better managing your time is worth it. Let your new knowledge be your guide. Good luck.